Freedom Cannot Rest:

Ella Baker

and the
Civil Rights Movement

Freedom Cannot Rest:

Ella Baker

and the
Civil Rights Movement

Lisa Frederiksen Bohannon

MORGAN
REYNOLDS
PUBLISHING

Greensboro, North Carolina

Portraits of
Black Americans

Bayard Rustin
A. Philip Randolph
Roy Wilkins
W. E. B. Du Bois
Gwendolyn Brooks
Marcus Garvey
William Grant Still
Richard Wright
Thurgood Marshall
Langston Hughes
John Coltrane

FREEDOM CANNOT REST:
ELLA BAKER AND THE CIVIL RIGHTS MOVEMENT

Copyright © 2005 by Lisa Frederiksen Bohannon

Library of Congress Cataloging-in-Publication Data

Bohannon, Lisa Frederiksen.
    Freedom cannot rest : Ella Baker and the civil rights movement / Lisa
    Frederiksen Bohannon.— 1st ed. p. cm.
Includes bibliographical references and index.
    ISBN-13: 978-1-931798-71-6 (library binding)
    ISBN-10: 1-931798-71-0 (library binding)
    1. Baker, Ella, 1903-1986. 2. Civil rights workers—United States—
Biography. 3. African American women civil rights workers—Biography. I.
Title.
    E185.97.B214B64 2005
    323'.092—dc22

                          2005007156

Printed in the United States of America
First Edition

Contents

Ella Baker. *(AP Photo)*

One

Deep Roots

Christened Ella Josephine Baker, Ella Jo, as she was known to her family, was born on December 13, 1903, in Norfolk, Virginia. She was named for her maternal grandmother, Elizabeth (Bet) Josephine Ross, who had been a house slave on a North Carolina plantation. According to Ella, when her grandmother was of marriageable age, "the mistress wanted to have her married to a man whom we knew as Uncle Carter . . . . And [Ella's grandmother] didn't like Carter. And so when she refused to concur with the wishes of the mistress, the mistress ordered her whipped, but the master, who was still her father, refused to have her whipped. . . . But he did put her out on the farm and she even had to plow . . . she would plow all day and dance all night. She was defiant."

Ella's grandmother, Bet Ross. *(Fundi: The Story of Ella Baker)*

Ella Jo inherited her grandmother's fighting spirit. When she was just six years old, her father took Ella and her brother, Curtis, to see Santa Claus. It was just before Christmas 1909, in downtown Norfolk. Slavery had ended less than fifty years before, and though the organization that would become the NAACP had been formed that very year, racism and discrimination pervaded the country, especially in the South.

Despite the widespread culture of racism, Ella's family was independent, successful, and proud. Even as a child she was used to being treated with respect, and she treated others the same way. It surprised her when a young white boy called her "nigger" on that December day, but she reacted to this all-too-common insult by whirling around and punching the boy. The next year, when the son of the white sheriff in Littleton, North Carolina, used the word, Ella chased him through the

Ella's grandfather, Mitchell Ross. *(Fundi: The Story of Ella Baker)*

yard, grabbed some rocks, and "started throwing [them] at him," she later said. Sometimes it was necessary to "fight back."

The Baker legacy of courage could be traced back through several generations. Grandmother Bet Ross learned to read during her time as a house slave. Many slaves did not learn to read, but Bet's master was also her father, which probably gave her more of a chance to improve herself. Bet, in turn, taught her husband, Ella's grandfather, Mitchell Ross, how to read. Ross was able to purchase some fifty acres of his former master's plantation in Warren County, North Carolina, following the Civil War. Other Ross family members did the same, and together they lived along the

The city of Norfolk, Virginia, at the turn of the century. *(Library of Congress)*

shores of the Roanoke River in the town called Littleton.

As literate landholders, Ella's grandparents were highly regarded in their community. They grew cotton, wheat, and corn; raised chickens and cows; and had an orchard, which meant there was always food on their table. More importantly, it meant the family was not dependent on the sharecropping system that character-ized the South after the Civil War. A significant number of former slaves (and poor whites) were sharecroppers on parcels of land that had been carved out of former plantations. Under this system the sharecropper, who did all of the work to plant, raise, and harvest the crop, had to "share" his crop with the landowner—typically about one-third to one-half of it. Sharecroppers rarely got ahead and most of them just scraped by. Ella's grandparents were generous with their bounty. They gave freely of their crops and loaned money, using their farm as collateral, to help their neighbors.

Ella's grandfather's literacy put him in a position to become the minister of the Roanoke Chapel Baptist Church, because he could read the Bible. Churches were the political, social, and economic heart and soul of most African-American communities in the South. The pastor was often the community's most highly regarded leader, as well as its teacher and business advisor.

Bet and Mitchell Ross passed along their work ethic and deep belief in the importance of education to their own children. They insisted their children attend school instead of working in the family's fields. Going to school allowed Georgianna, Ella's mother, to become a teacher in Littleton before marrying Ella's father, Blake Baker, in 1896, the same year as the *Plessy v. Ferguson* Supreme Court decision.

In an eight-to-one ruling, the U.S. Supreme Court ruled in *Plessy v. Ferguson* that the Fourteenth Amendment, which was added to the Constitution after the Civil War, did not intend "to enforce social as distinguished from political . . . equality, or a commingling of the two races upon terms unsatisfactory to each other." In other words, it was legal to pass laws to require "separate" facilities for African Americans and whites as long as the facilities were "equal." This became known as the "separate but equal" doctrine, and while it originally applied to train cars, southern state legislatures and local city and county governments soon passed laws that made it apply to restaurants, theaters, cemeteries, neighborhoods, churches, restrooms, courtrooms, juries, and public schools. These laws were dubbed Jim Crow laws,

JIM CROW

Minstrel shows, a popular entertainment at the turn of the century, featured white performers wearing burnt cork or greasepaint and performing routines that ridiculed African Americans. Jim Crow was a popular minstrel show character, and his name came to represent the segregation of the South.

Jim Crow laws were similar to the Black Codes that had been enacted in 1865 after the Civil War and the Thirteenth Amendment had freed nearly four million slaves. Though they varied from state to state, Black Codes imposed unfair restrictions on former slaves to keep them poor, illiterate, and subservient to whites. The codes were passed by legislative bodies dominated by members of the Democratic Party. In the South after the Civil War, the Democratic Party emerged as the political force for white supremacy.

At the end of the Civil War, the federal government faced two challenges: how to integrate the states that had seceded back into the Union, and how to integrate the newly freed slaves into society. Much of the economy and landscape of the South was in ruins. At the time, Congress, controlled by Republicans who felt strongly that the power structure of the South needed to be changed, passed several pieces of legislation and three constitutional amendments in an effort to rebuild the nation and provide and protect the civil rights of former slaves.

The Freedmen's Bureau of 1866 oversaw reconstruction programs, especially the opening of some 3,000 schools, technical and industrial institutions, and colleges to educate former slaves. The Civil Rights Acts of 1866 protected African Americans from unfair laws, while the Fourteenth Amendment (passed in 1866, ratified in 1868) granted citizenship to "all persons born or naturalized in the United States." The First Reconstruction Act of 1867 divided the southern states into five military districts led by generals who took direction from General Ulysses S. Grant, who in turn took direction from the president. The Fifteenth Amendment (passed in 1869, ratified in 1870) guaranteed the right to vote to all male citizens, including former slaves. Finally, the Enforcement Acts of 1870 and 1871 authorized federal troops to halt the activities of groups violating these laws, including the Ku Klux Klan.

Reconstruction lasted for about eleven years, and during that time more than 700,000 African Americans registered to vote and succeeded in helping elect African-American congressmen, state legislators, and local government officials. Between 1867 and 1870, African-American voters outnumbered white voters in South Carolina, Alabama, Florida, Mississippi, and Louisiana. African American literacy rates went from 7 percent in 1865 to 44 percent in 1890. Former slaves, such as Ella Baker's maternal grandparents, forged new lives for themselves and their families.

The Compromise of 1877 was the result of the disputed 1876 presidential election between Rutherford B. Hayes, the Republican candidate, and Samuel L. Tilden, the Democratic candidate. Tilden had led the popular vote in the election, but the legality of ballots from four states was questioned. To resolve the dispute, Congress set up an electoral commission, which in the end awarded the presidency to Hayes in exchange for an agreement that effectively ended Reconstruction, a major concession to southern Democrats. Without the protection of federal troops, conditions in the South for African Americans returned to a nearly pre-Civil War state. The 1896 *Plessy v. Ferguson* ruling was the final victory for segregationists in the southern states and provided the legal foundation for passage and enforcement of laws very similar to the old Black Codes.

named for the popular minstrel song "Jump, Jim Crow," and they effectively legalized segregation.

Jim Crow laws permeated all social interactions between white and black people. Many of the racial distinctions intended to remind African Americans of their second-class status were enforced in the North as well as in the South. African-American men could not shake hands with white men because it suggested they were equal; African-American men could not offer their hand to or look directly at a white woman; African Americans could not eat with whites unless conditions forced them to, in which case whites were served first and a partition was erected between them; African Americans were given curfews in some areas and had to be off the streets by a certain time, often as early as 6:00 PM; African-American men and women could not show public affection for one another; African Americans were expected to look at the ground when addressing whites and to step aside or off the sidewalk when passing a white person; African Americans always had to address whites as Mr., Mrs., Miss, Ma'am, or Sir, but whites never addressed African Americans as anything other than their first name, "boy," "auntie," or "nigger"; African Americans could not enter a store if a white person was in it, and if a white person entered, the white person was served first; and African Americans could not try on clothing before buying it because whites refused to wear anything an African-American person had worn.

The penalties imposed on African Americans and

A representation of the minstrel figure Jim Crow. *(Library of Congress)*

whites that violated Jim Crow laws could be severe. If the local sheriff did not enforce the laws, the Ku Klux Klan often did. Churches and schools were burned; teachers, professionals, landowners, and businessmen were beaten or whipped; women and children could be raped or brutalized without consequences. Even if a Klansman was arrested for one of these horrific crimes, they were seldom found guilty because only white men were allowed to sit on juries.

Jim Crow laws and etiquette and the whites' subjec-

W. E. B. Du Bois. *(Courtesy of Art Resource)*

tive enforcement practices forced most African Americans to live dual lives—one among other African Americans and another when among whites. Some described this dual life as "putting on the face." W. E. B. Du Bois, one of the most influential African-American leaders of the time, described it as "two-ness" or being "born with a veil." Du Bois's description of two-ness was published in 1903, the year Ella Baker was born, in his collection of essays, *The Souls of Black Folk*. He wrote, "It is a peculiar sensation, this double-consciousness, this sense of always looking at one's self through the eyes of others, of measuring one's soul by the tape of a world that looks on in amused contempt and pity. One ever feels his two-ness— an American, a Negro; two souls, two thoughts, two unreconciled strivings; two warring ideals in one dark body, whose dogged strength alone keeps it from being torn asunder."

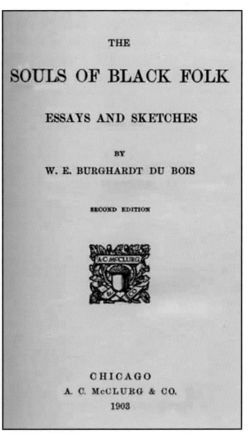

THE

SOULS OF BLACK FOLK

ESSAYS AND SKETCHES

BY

W. E. BURGHARDT DU BOIS

SECOND EDITION

CHICAGO
A. C. McCLURG & CO.
1903

The title page of Du Bois's groundbreaking book, *The Souls of Black Folk.*

Du Bois helped found the interracial National Association for the Advancement of Colored People (NAACP) on February 12, 1909—the hundredth anniversary of Abraham Lincoln's birthday. The NAACP vowed "to achieve, through peaceful and lawful means, equal citizenship rights for all American citizens by eliminating segregation and discrimination in housing, employment, voting, schools, the courts, transportation, recreation."

Du Bois graduated from Fisk University in 1888 and went on to receive his PhD in history from Harvard University. He rose to prominence in part because of his opposition to Booker T. Washington, the best known African-American leader at the turn of the twentieth century. A former slave, Washington became president of the Tuskegee Institute in 1881 and dedicated his life to making it one of the leading higher educational institutions for African Americans in the United States.

Washington believed that African Americans should take a more gradual approach toward ending discrimination and should first concentrate on elevating themselves economically: "The wisest among my race understand that agitation for social equality is an extremist folly. It is important and right that all privileges of the law be ours but it is vastly more important that we be prepared for the exercise of those privileges." Washington believed that African Americans should enroll in technical or industrial training schools, like the Tuskegee Institute, as opposed to getting a college or university degree. There they could learn a trade, like better farming techniques, carpentry, or brick making for men, and practical things like sewing, cooking, and housekeeping for women. With this kind of training and the subsequent economic success it would bring, Washington believed African Americans would be in a position to prove to whites

Tuskegee Institute founder Booker T. Washington. *(Library of Congress)*

they were their equals and deserving of their respect.

Du Bois agreed, in part, with Washington's conten-
tion "that in the great leap from slavery to freedom we
may overlook the fact that the masses of us are to live
by the productions of our hands," but he was also of the
opinion that a small group, which he called "the Talented
Tenth," needed a quality scholastic education (not technical training) in order to become leaders who could
forge a path for others to follow. Du Bois said, "The
Negro race, like all races, is going to be saved by its
exceptional men. The problem of education, then, among

Negroes must first of all deal with the Talented Tenth; it is the problem of developing the Best of this race that they may guide the Mass away from the contamination and death of the Worst, in their own and other races." Du Bois believed that the achievements of the Talented Tenth would be so powerful as to destroy stereotypes and end racial discrimination more quickly.

The seeds of what would become the civil rights movement had been sown by the founding of the NAACP and were soon nourished by the development of industries, even in the mostly rural South, which drew many African Americans to the cities to find work and, hopefully, better lives.

As a young couple, Ella's parents moved to Norfolk, Virginia, the big city nearest to Littleton and the first to change from horse-drawn trolley cars to electric cars. It had a population of some 50,000 people. Norfolk was a racially segregated city, but Ella's parents hoped the opportunities there would outweigh the Jim Crow challenges they would face. Ella's father found good work as a waiter on the ferryboat between the port cities of Norfolk and Washington, D.C.

Ella's parents moved into a big house in a newly developed "colored" neighborhood where their first child, Blake Curtis, was born. He was Georgianna's third pregnancy; the other two had ended in miscarriages or stillbirths. One more stillbirth preceded Ella, who was followed by the Bakers' last child, Margaret (called Maggie).

Ella's mother was occupied with the children, the two

Ella's mother, Georgianna. *(Fundi: The Story of Ella Baker)*

borders they had taken in, and tending to the sick in their neighborhood. Her father worked twenty-four-hour shifts on the ferryboat. Ella described her parents as being very different from one another. Her father was easygoing: "He was the one you would depend on to take you to the zoo." Her mother, on the other hand, was very strict. If Ella and her sibling got too rambunctious, her mother would reprimand them saying theirs "was a work house, not a play house."

Ella spent summers on the family farm in Littleton with her maternal grandparents, siblings, and mother, while her father stayed behind in Norfolk to work. She would travel throughout Warren County with her grandfather in his horse-drawn buggy as he delivered guest sermons at one church after another. Along the way he told her stories about their family's legacy of courage:

"[In] my grandpa's community there was this sense of independence. . . . When they were beginning to permit the Negroes to vote after Emancipation, he and his sons got into quite a battle with somebody who called him 'nigger.' You see, they would fight back. Now, whether this was good or bad . . . it provided you with a sense of your own worth and you weren't brow beaten."

By the time Ella was seven, in 1910, her mother was anxious to return to Littleton year round. Her health was poor and Ella's grandfather had died the year before, leaving her grandmother to manage the family farm alone. The opportunities in Norfolk had not materialized the way she had hoped. The influx of African Americans had strained Norfolk's racial tensions to a breaking point. Jim Crow laws were strictly enforced. Signs reading "No Dogs, No Negroes" appeared in restaurant and shop windows. When the black boxer Jack Johnson defeated a white opponent, race riots swept the city.

Ella's parents decided to split the family to escape this environment, though they never divorced. Ella, her siblings, and her mother moved to Littleton, while her father stayed in Norfolk to continue working. Ella kept in touch with her father with letters and the occasional weekend or holiday visit, but her mother and grandmother would now become the central figures in her life.

Two

Littleton

As Ella later described it, "There was a deep sense of community [in Littleton]. . . . If there were emergencies, the farmer next to you would share in something to meet the emergency." She added, "There was no sense of social hierarchy in terms of those who have, having the right to look down upon, or to evaluate as a lesser breed, those who didn't have. . . . Plus . . . [we had] the 'Christian' concept of sharing with others. . . . Your relationship to human beings was far more important than your relationship to the amount of money that you made." Like their neighbors, Ella and her siblings joined her mother and grandmother in caring for whoever needed help, whether it was food, clothing, nursing, baby-sitting, or sharing farm equipment.

"We were the kind of family that was not just my

mother and her brood, but if somebody came by who needed something, you got something," said Ella. She later recalled getting up "[m]any a night . . . in the middle of the night when somebody knocked at the door. The train had brought somebody who was coming in either to a marriage or funeral. . . . The first thing . . . you would ask if they wanted to eat something. If necessary, we'd get up and make a fire and heat up the food that was left over. Whatever was necessary to make people comfortable."

The following year, Ella's mother rented her family a roomy home of their own. She dedicated a great deal of time to church work. She was an auxiliary to the National Baptist Convention and a member of the National Woman's Convention, a church community service organization much like the National Association of Colored Women (NACW), founded in 1896. These organizations challenged negative stereotypes of African-American women and provided a means for groups of African-American women to help those less fortunate.

The National Woman's Convention sponsored orphanages, raised funds for kindergartens, fought for temperance, worked with the sick and elderly, fought for antilynching legislation, sought an end to segregation, and raised funds for scholarships for African-American college students and for church-affiliated elementary schools. Watching her mother and the other women at their convention meetings handle all business and financial matters without a man's input or help gave Ella

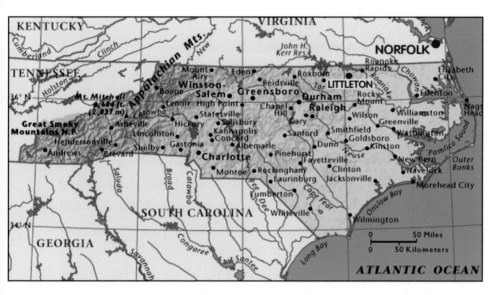

Littleton, North Carolina, where Ella moved with her mother in 1910, is located approximately 115 miles southwest of Norfolk, Virginia, where Ella was born.

an appreciation for women's capabilities to serve in important leadership roles.

Littleton was populated predominately by African Americans. "The manner in which we lived sheltered us from the bad aspects of race," Ella said. "We did not come in contact with whites too much. . . . I was shielded from having contact with them at an early age. . . . This was a complete black community to a large extent. Even the store on the corner, it was Mr. Foreman's store, he was black. . . . So, this [was] the kind of insulation that was provided by the African American people themselves. . . . You didn't have to run afoul of a lot of insults."

The African-American children in Littleton had it somewhat better than most. Most public schools for white children had adequate teachers, the latest textbooks, desks, school supplies, doors, glass windows, and heat. Public schools for African-American children, as with everything else in the Jim Crow South, were grossly inferior. Public spending on education in many southern regions was around ten dollars per African-American student as compared to $250 per white student. Littleton's two-room black elementary school was attached to the South Street Baptist Church and funded by church donations. It provided instruction for all who could attend, from sharecroppers' children to more fortunate children like Ella and her siblings. But Ella's mother didn't leave anything to chance. She taught her children to read before they started school and, once they were enrolled, she assigned her own homework on top of their school homework. By the time Ella was ten, she had already read the Bible at least twice. The daughter of one of the sharecroppers remembered, "[W]e went to school when we could, but papa was on somebody else's land so we had to work the fields when he needed us. . . . Ella Jo and them went to school regular through, and their mama taught them at home too."

Few African-American children obtained a high school education in public schools. Mississippi, South Carolina, North Carolina, and Louisiana, for example, did not have a single public high school for African-American students in 1915. But Ella's parents were determined their children would continue their education and sent all three to private boarding schools.

Georgianna Baker wanted Ella to attend Shaw Academy and University in Raleigh, North Carolina. Shaw had been founded during Reconstruction by the American Baptist Home Mission as the Baptist Institution for Negroes and had an impeccable reputation.

Ella spent much of her last year at home "largely with an old time teacher. . . . I went through all this business with grammar that I couldn't even articulate now . . . [but] that teacher was just like my mother. . . . She carried me through all the parts of speech and how they [were] used." Ella later acknowledged that her proficiency in the written and spoken word was the result of the preparation she got that year, and that it gave her a great deal of self-confidence and enhanced her effectiveness as a writer and public speaker.

Ella Baker entered Shaw Academy and University just before her fifteenth birthday, in 1918. She would call it home for the next nine years. Admissions materials stated that applicants had to be of "unblemished moral character" and that "only those students who [were] willing to comply cheerfully with reasonable rules and regulations [were] desired at [the] institution." Conduct was strictly regulated: there could be "no frivolous conversations or attention to trivial matters or visiting in each others rooms, lounging upon beds or loitering upon the grounds."

Shaw provided Baker with an experience she had not dreamed possible. She studied literature and philosophy and read Immanuel Kant, Socrates, and Aristotle. She studied biographies of African Americans and learned

Ella attended Shaw Academy and University in Raleigh, North Carolina, from 1918 to 1927.

of her people's deep, rich history through the lives of Frederick Douglass, the famous African-American abolitionist and advisor to president Lincoln during the Civil War; Harriet Tubman, who was credited with aiding some three hundred slaves in their escape to freedom via the Underground Railroad; and Sojourner Truth, a renowned orator and writer who traveled extensively to speak in favor of abolition and women's rights.

Baker loved sciences, excelling in biology and chemistry, and was chosen to work as a lab assistant to the chemistry professor. She also participated on the debate team and, according to one team member, "helped to win a lot of trophies and honors for the school."

Baker's most influential mentor was Professor Benjamin Brawley. Brawley taught Shakespeare, coached the debate team, and was the faculty advisor for the campus newspaper, the *Shaw University Journal.* Brawley freely expressed his abhorrence for the second-class status imposed on African Americans as the consequence of Jim Crow laws and Jim Crow etiquette. Brawley also encouraged Baker to write for the *Journal*, and she became the youngest contributing writer, publishing articles during her freshman year of college. She went on to serve as the paper's associate editor in 1924, and editor in chief the following year.

Shaw University exposed Baker to a larger world through the influence of international students from Canada, Mexico, Liberia, Panama, the Philippines, Puerto Rico, South Africa, Sierra Leone, the Congo, and Jamaica. None were white. Visiting speakers further broadened her world.

During her senior year of high school, Baker's fellow students asked her to represent them in petitioning the university to relax one of its restrictive dress codes so they could wear silk stockings—the latest fashion craze. Baker agreed and wrote a letter requesting a change in the student dress code, not because she wanted to wear silk stockings herself but because she "felt it was their right to wear stockings if they wanted to." The dean of women was aghast and assigned the students extra hours in chapel to pray for enlightenment to correct their thinking. When Baker appeared before the dean, she said, "I didn't seem particularly penitent, and she [the dean] was very disturbed about it. But it didn't bother me because I felt I was correct."

Baker took another stand when she refused to participate in singing African-American spirituals for the white benefactors from the North who visited the campus. Baker considered it kowtowing to those who held power. She apparently suffered no consequence for her refusal to sing.

In addition to her first exposure to activism, her well-rounded academic education, and her appreciation for the world at large, Baker also credited Shaw with giving her the tools and self-confidence to challenge the "contradictions in what was said and what was done," and to stand up as a woman in a man's world. "My man-woman relationships were on the basis of just being a human being, not a sex object. As far as my sense of security, it had been established. . . . I had been able to compete on levels such as scholarship. . . . And I could stand my own in debate," said Baker. She did not date while at Shaw. One of her classmates explained: "You know how men were at the time, and some of them still today, they wanted you to be beautiful and dumb. [She] was too intelligent for that. The boys were probably intimidated."

At the age of twenty-three, in April 1927, Baker was

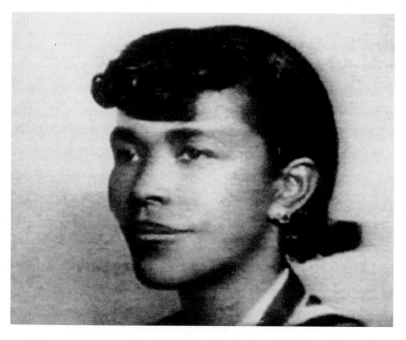

Ella Baker in her mid-twenties. *(Jackie Brockington)*

valedictorian of her graduating class from Shaw University—the same honor she had received when graduating from Shaw Academy. Her parents were in the audience as she took the podium and called for social justice and grassroots activism: "Awake youth of the land and accept this noble challenge of salvaging the strong ship of civilization, by the anchors of right, justice and love. . . . We will strike against evil, strife and war until the echo shall resound in the recesses of the earth."

Finances kept Baker from becoming a medical missionary or pursuing graduate studies in social work at the University of Chicago. She refused to become a teacher. As she explained it, African-American women "couldn't teach unless somebody in the white hierarchy okayed your teaching." For Baker, this made teaching "a demeaning sort of thing, and I resented this, and I refused to teach." Instead, Baker turned her sights on New York City. She had a cousin, Martha, raised by Ella's mother, who lived there with her husband. With Georgianna's reluctant blessing, Ella Baker moved to New York City.

Three

Harlem

Ella Baker arrived in New York City some five months after her graduation from college. She was immediately drawn to the vibrant world of Harlem. Named after the town of Haarlem in the Netherlands by the original Dutch settlers of Manhattan Island in the mid-1600s, Harlem had become home to a significant number of African Americans during the first quarter of the twentieth century. Between 1910 and 1930, the African-American population of Harlem jumped from roughly 91,000 to over 300,000.

The internal migration, also known as the Great Migration, from the Jim Crow South to northern cities like New York was spurred by African Americans seeking employment in the northern factories that grew and expanded as a result of World War I and by the experi-

In the early decades of the twentieth century, Harlem quickly became a center of cultural and political activity for the African-American community. This painting by Edward Burra conveys some of the vitality of the neighborhood. *(Smithsonian Museum of American Art, Washington, D.C.)*

ences of some 200,000 African Americans who had served their country during the war (albeit in segregated units). Instead of returning home to the Jim Crow South, many of them opted to seek greater freedom in the North. One African American veteran explained: "Try to imagine, if you can, the feelings of a Negro army officer, who clothed in the full panoply of his profession and wearing the decorations for valor of three governments, is forced to the indignity of a Jim Crow car and who is refused a seat in a theatre and a bed in a hotel. . . . Think of the feelings in the hearts of boys and girls of my race who are clean, intelligent and industrious who apply for positions only to meet with the reply, 'We don't hire niggers.'"

Once she had settled in with her cousin, Baker set out to find a job. She experienced rejection not just because of her race but also because of her gender. The secluded worlds of Littleton and Shaw had not prepared Baker for this reality, but she persevered and eventually found a job as a waitress at New York University's Judson House in Greenwich Village.

In the late 1920s, Greenwich Village and Harlem were two of the most politically and socially active communities in the country. Harlem was populated mostly by African Americans and was in the midst of a cultural blossoming. Musicians, poets, writers, and artists of all sorts made Harlem a place described as "exotic, colorful, and sensuous; a place of laughing, singing, and dancing; a place where life wakes up at night." It also made Harlem a place of opportunity, pride, and hope for African Americans across the country. The NAACP's journal, *The Crisis*, edited by W. E. B. Du Bois as part of his persistent campaign to develop the Talented Tenth, brought the news of Harlem's flowering to African Americans across the country, inspiring them with stories about the achievements of their race.

Greenwich Village was home to bohemian intellectuals, many of them immigrants from Eastern Europe, and had a reputation for radicalism. In the Village, Baker found herself in the thick of social and political debates as she waited tables, served meals, and refilled coffee cups during her breakfast and lunch shifts. Much of the conversation centered on the philosophy of communism and the 1917 Bolshevik revolution in Russia. Led by Vladimir Ilyich Lenin, the Bolsheviks had overthrown

Vladimir Lenin, Communist leader of the Bolshevik revolution in Russia.

the czarist government and implemented a Communist regime. Communism stresses the elimination of private property and aims to equalize society by giving owner-ship of goods and means of production to the people as a whole. After Lenin's death in 1924, control of Com-munist Russia—officially called the Union of Soviet Socialist Republics—was assumed by Joseph Stalin. He was opposed by Lenin's supporter Leon Trotsky, but Stalin engineered Trotsky's exile in 1928.

Stalin's plan to create "socialism in one country"—Russia alone—was undertaken with repressive and aggressive measures, angering those who saw their dreams of a truly Communist state disappear under Stalin's totalitarian regime. The question was whether Stalin had diverted true communism with his policies, or was repression an inevitable result in a Communist system? Many who escaped from the Soviet Union, and others who were attracted by the Communist ideal, gathered in Greenwich Village, where they argued the pros and cons of education, cooperatives, and labor unions. Baker was fascinated by the discussions and was eager to extend her education past the limitations of Shaw University. She spent time between shifts reading in the Forty-second Street and Schomburg libraries, or on the street, talking to people about how to change the world.

Socialists believed in many of the same tenets of communism, but argued for slower, more evolutionary change instead of sudden, violent change. Socialist philosophy intrigued Baker. Since the end of the Civil War, a spirit of progressive reform had taken hold of many Americans. People like Jane Addams of Hull House raised awareness about the plight of the poor in urban areas. Suffragettes like Susan B. Anthony fought for women to have the right to vote, which did not come until 1920. The forming of the NAACP sent the message that African Americans were wearying of their second-class status. Socialism promised a means to achieve all these goals—it held out the hope of a classless society in which each person would be rewarded according to his or her needs. Because socialism rejected the idea of a hierarchy, it was especially appealing to those people at the bottom of their society—those who suffered dis- crimination and mistreatment.

The Great Migration that followed WWI had caused a political shift in northern American cities. For the first time since Reconstruction, there were concentrated pockets of African Americans who could actually reg- ister and vote as a bloc and have an impact on elections. Baker saw the potential in this newfound empowerment and set out to learn about the political issues of the day. "I went everywhere there was discussion," she said. "New York was not as hazardous as it now is. You could walk the streets at three in the morning. And so wherever there was a discussion, I'd go. . . . And maybe I was the only woman or the only black, it didn't matter. . . . You see, New York was the hotbed of—let's call it radical thinking. . . . Boy, it was *good*, stimulating!"

Asa Philip Randolph in 1912. *(Library of Congress)*

Baker was most intrigued by the discussions about A. Philip Randolph, Chandler Owen, and Marcus Garvey. Owen and Randolph were known in Harlem as Lenin and Trotsky. A. Philip Randolph was a socialist, and the president and founder of the Brotherhood of Sleeping Car Porters, the first labor union for African Americans. Its members were the porters and workers on railroad sleeping cars. Randolph had succeeded in getting the Brotherhood accepted into the American Federation of Labor (AFL) at a time when over half of the AFL's union affiliates barred African Americans from their membership ranks. Chandler Owen was also a member of the Socialist Party and, together with Randolph, had co-

The flamboyant and controversial leader of the Back-to-Africa movement, Marcus Garvey. (Library of Congress)

founded the magazine *The Messenger,* in 1917.

Marcus Garvey had organized the Universal Negro Improvement Association (UNIA) in 1914, and in 1920 convened its first convention in New York City. Garvey's convention audience had been taken by his plan for African Americans to escape the racism of the United States by returning to the land of their ancestors. Garvey followed that convention with a tour of the United States and the publishing of his book *The Negro World.* His Back-to-Africa movement, as it was called, resonated with African Americans, and it wasn't long before UNIA boasted tens of thousands of members across the country. By the time Baker arrived on the scene in Harlem, Garvey had been deported to Jamaica, his birthplace, in lieu of completing a prison sentence for mail fraud. The enthusiasm and pride he had stirred up, however, remained.

Two hotbeds of Harlem political activity that Baker frequented were the 135th Street Library and the Harlem YWCA. The Harlem YWCA was a gathering place for young, single women, many of them, like Baker, drawn to Harlem for its political, cultural, and social stimulation. Baker met one woman there, Pauli Murray, who would become a life-long friend and fellow activist in the civil rights movement. Murray believed that women were as capable as men and shared with Baker a deep-founded abhorrence of oppression in any form. In the years to come, she and Baker would discover that the civil rights movement was as male-dominated an institution as any other in the country.

Pauli Murray.

Together with Murray and other women from the YWCA, Baker attended lectures and discussion programs held at the 135th Street Library, where she met Ernestine Rose. Rose, a white librarian, was twenty years Baker's senior. She was one of the many people who proved you did not have to be black to hate prejudice, and you did not have to be a victim of injustice to fight against it. She had founded the Negro Division in the library. Baker and Rose established the Negro History Club, which hosted rousing forums to discuss historical and current topics of importance to African Americans. They paid soapbox speakers to incite participation in these discussions—a tradition brought to Harlem by Caribbean immigrants. "If you hadn't stood on the corner of 135th and 7th Avenue [protesting and debating] . . . you weren't with it," said Baker.

Baker joined the staff of a weekly newspaper, the *American West Indian News*, at the age of twenty-six, and the *Negro National News*, published by George Schuyler, a socialist and leading African-American intellectual, a year later. She also wrote articles for a number of other publications, such as the *Amsterdam News*, for much of twentieth century one of the leading weekly newspapers run by African Americans, the *National News,* and the NAACP's *The Crisis.*

Then, almost overnight, the Harlem Renaissance began to unravel. The stock market crashed on October 24, 1929, and millions of Americans lost their homes and life savings in the wake of the bank failures that followed. By 1932, more than thirteen million Americans were unemployed. The Great Depression would last until the late 1930s.

People could no longer afford to spend money on arts, literature, or nightlife, forcing many of Harlem's night-clubs to close. Newspapers, recording companies, and publishers folded as well. The economic, cultural, and social inroads made by the Harlem Renaissance came to a halt, and the pall that replaced them sent a demoral-izing shudder through African Americans across the country.

Political activism in Harlem picked up steam during

George Schuyler. *(Library of Congress)*

the Great Depression, however. Baker began working with George Schuyler, who wrote a column, "Views & Reviews," for the *Pittsburgh Courier*. In one article he described how Harlem families could use their collective buying power to purchase food in order to survive the Great Depression's effects. He called it "economic salvation."

Schuyler and Baker set out to put this idea in action by forming the Young Negroes' Cooperative League (YNCL) in 1930. Its goal was to help African Americans "gain economic power through consumer cooperation" by organizing local community cooperative councils across the country. Individuals would pool their money in order to purchase foods and other goods in large quantities at a low cost. They would use their savings "for the common good" by investing in "clinics, libraries, and cooperative housing to combat slums." Baker and Schuyler believed economic planning would form the basis for the "second emancipation" of African Americans. They also believed that young people should lead the effort because young people were not as demoralized by years of experience with Jim Crow.

Baker created several programs and brochures to provide guidance to the local cooperative councils, and planned and executed a nationwide tour to train local leaders to be grassroots organizers. As the call for sponsorships of this tour explained, Baker wanted to "awaken the Negro consumer to the ENORMOUS POWER that is his as a consumer; . . . as an antidote to some of the hopelessness with which the inarticulate masses of Black Americans face the question, 'After the Depression, What?'" To do this, the call went on to explain, "Miss Baker will spend at least two days in your community, studying with you your problems, organizing groups where there are none, pointing out from the experiences of others what plans to make and what steps to avoid."

Eventually there were some two dozen YNCL councils. Each operated independently but contributed a portion of their proceeds to the national office in New York City. Baker served as YNCL's unpaid executive director. In 1932, at the age of twenty-eight, she launched a three-month fund-raising program that she called Penny a Day. The campaign urged every YNCL participant to set aside a penny a day for the good of the whole.

Unfortunately, the YNCL, like many organizations during the Depression, was not able to overcome its financial obstacles and was forced to dissolve. Baker continued to work in a series of short-term jobs with community groups such as the Boosters and Friends of Africa for the World's Fair, the Youth Committee of 100 Against Lynching, and the Brotherhood of Sleeping Car Porters. She also got paid as a freelancer to write for a variety of publications. She would continue to take these kinds of positions throughout her life in order to support herself while volunteering the majority of her time to grassroots activism.

About this same time, Baker moved out of her cousin's

apartment and into her own one-bedroom apartment in Harlem. She was hired by the 135th Street Library and in 1936, at the age of thirty-two, created the Young People's Forum (YPF)—an organization for Harlem's youth. The purpose of YPF was to expose Harlem's young people, ages sixteen to twenty-six, to the world of books and critical thinking through discussions on controversial "social, economic, and cultural topics." She relished her job—it involved young people and their education. She also worked with the Mothers in the Park program and the Harlem Adult Education Committee—both had goals similar to the YPF, except their targeted participants were parents.

By this time, Baker was something of an expert in consumer affairs, grassroots organizing, and develop-

Franklin Delano Roosevelt, thirty-second president of the United States. *(Library of Congress)*

ing effective educational programs. Her talents made her an excellent choice to be hired as a consumer education teacher for the Workers Education Project (WEP) under the Works Progress Administration (WPA). The WPA was one of President Franklin Roosevelt's New Deal programs, begun after he took office in 1933 to provide relief, create jobs, and stimulate the economy during the Great Depression.

There were approximately one thousand teachers from across the nation in the WEP program who were charged with holding consumer education classes at the grassroots level—in settlement houses, union halls, churches, and workplaces—in cooperation with the local leaders: union officials, ministers, businessmen, and other community leaders. Baker wrote several educational publications that were used in these consumer education classes. "The main objective," she explained, "is to aid the consumer to a more intelligent understanding of the social and political economy of which he is a part." Baker was made the assistant project supervisor in the Manhattan WEP office and worked there with Pauli Murray.

President Roosevelt's New Deal programs were controversial. His second term saw something of a backlash against his policies. Many conservatives thought he spent too much effort trying to help the poor. Some of his programs were struck down by the Supreme Court. But Roosevelt, urged on by his wife, Eleanor, was determined to advance his agenda. Eleanor Roosevelt was

Walter White. *(Library of Congress)*

also an avowed advocate for racial justice. She met often with black leaders A. Philip Randolph, Walter White, and Mary McLeod Bethune.

Walter White had joined the NAACP in 1918 as one of its chief investigators of race crimes. He achieved success in part because his light complexion and blue eyes allowed him to mix easily with whites while pursuing his investigations, the results of which he published in *The Crisis* and elsewhere. White became executive director of the NAACP in 1931 and the undisputed leader of the NAACP when W. E. B. Du Bois resigned in 1934.

Mary McLeod Bethune, another member of President Roosevelt's so-called Black Cabinet, was one of seventeen children born to former slaves. She went on to graduate from college with a degree in education. Bethune had founded the Daytona Normal and Industrial School for Negro Girls, which later merged with the nearby

Mary McLeod Bethune while president of Bethune-Cookman College in Daytona, Florida. *(Library of Congress)*

boys' school and became Bethune-Cookman College, located in Daytona, Florida. She founded the National Council of Negro Women in 1935 as an "organization of organizations" banding together "to advance opportunities and the quality of life for African American women, their families and communities." Bethune gained national recognition in 1936, when President Roosevelt appointed her director of the division of Negro affairs of the National Youth Administration and special adviser on minority affairs.

A. Philip Randolph was another member of Roosevelt's Black Cabinet. In 1941, he convinced the president to sign Executive Order 8802 by threatening a march on Washington, D.C., to demand the government's integration of the military and equal employment opportunities for African Americans in the defense industries. Although Roosevelt's Executive Order did not integrate the military itself, it did set up a Fair Employment Practices Committee to ensure equal hiring opportunities for African Americans in the defense industries, marking the first time a president had taken action to prevent employment discrimination against African Americans.

In the years ahead, Baker would work with these people in the struggle to end Jim Crow laws and secure equal civil rights for all African Americans.

In 1939 or 1940, Ella Baker married a man she had known for many years, T. J. (Bob) Roberts. He had stayed in Littleton when she moved to New York, and despite the ups and downs of a long-distance relationship, they had remained committed to each other. Roberts had been a member of the Brotherhood of Sleeping Car Porters before he took a job traveling as a refrigeration mechanic and was described as gentle and kind but, as one blunt observer put it, "out of his league with Ella." One of Baker's political associates who knew them well said, "She took him in like a little puppy out of the rain. I think she sort of felt sorry for him." Another friend said, "He had his interests and she had hers."

Once married, the couple set up their home in an apartment in Harlem. Baker kept her own name, saying, "I had it all this time, I just figured I would keep it."

Baker was far more politically active than her husband, although both traveled extensively with their jobs and joined forces to work for their apartment building's tenant association. Her marriage was always very private. One student later recalled, "It was one of the few things she just wouldn't talk about." Another said, "Many people didn't even know Miss Baker had ever been married; she was explicitly *Miss* Baker." In later years, interviewers who broached the subject of Baker's marriage were politely encouraged to ask another question.

Baker's Harlem experiences, upbringing in Littleton, and experiences at Shaw had set her focus on education, grassroots organizing, and activism. Henceforth, she was determined to use those experiences to "relate to people and share whatever capacity I have to help them to use [their own] capacities" to fight their own battles, one issue at a time.

Four

The NAACP

In December of 1941, Baker was hired to work as an assistant field secretary for the NAACP. Her salary was twenty-nine dollars a week. The NAACP had made significant strides during the 1930s under the executive directorship of Walter White. Its efforts to pass anti-lynching and antisegregation legislation were expanded into a long-range strategic plan to use the legal system to chip away at segregation. Charles Hamilton Houston formed the NAACP's Legal Defense Committee in 1934 and then hired Thurgood Marshall, who would successfully argue the *Brown v. Board of Education* case before the Supreme Court, which overturned the *Plessy v. Ferguson* doctrine of "separate and equal." Marshall established the NAACP Legal Defense and Education Fund to support teams of NAACP lawyers who traveled

Thurgood Marshall during his early days working as an attorney for the NAACP. *(Library of Congress)*

to take on hundreds of cases at the local, state, and national levels. The cases challenged discrimination and segregation in employment, travel, housing, education, legal systems, jails, prisons, and politics.

Two such cases were *Powell v. Alabama* (the Scottsboro Nine case) and *Gaines v. Canada.* The so-called Scottsboro "Boys" were nine young African Americans who had been accused of raping two white women. In a one-day trial, in a courtroom dominated by an angry mob, they had been found guilty and sentenced to death. The NAACP took the case to the Supreme Court, which, in *Powell v. Alabama,* held that they had not received due process in accordance with the Fourteenth Amendment and thus should be freed from prison. In *Gaines v. Canada,* the Supreme Court ruled that all-white graduate schools had to integrate or build "separate but equal" graduate schools for African-American students. This was the first time the "but equal" portion of the *Plessy v. Ferguson* doctrine had been upheld.

Assistant secretaries like Baker provided the link between the national NAACP office and the local branches. They helped local branch leaders recruit new

The case of the Scottsboro defendants deeply affected many Americans. This print, from the cover of a booklet created to raise money for the Scottsboro Defense Fund, was made by a white artist named Prentiss Taylor. The booklet, entitled "Scottsboro Limited," included four poems and a play in verse by Harlem Renaissance writer Langston Hughes. *(Library of Congress)*

members and conduct fund-raising drives. Baker wanted very much "to place the NAACP and its program on the lips of all the people," and traveled a grueling schedule for six months of the year. Between February 11 and July 8, 1942, for example, she met with "thirty-eight branches and [addressed] 178 different groups . . . in the States of Florida, Alabama, Georgia, Virginia and North Carolina."

The work Baker did was dangerous and difficult. Much of the time she traveled alone, riding in segregated cars on trains and in the back of buses. When she judged the situation safe enough, she made her own small stands against Jim Crow. She might test a bus driver by taking a seat on the edge of the whites-only section or ask to be served in a railroad car where white people were eating. But much of the time she had to swallow insults and indignities in the interest of achieving her greater goals. Many white southerners considered the NAACP to be a militant organization, and asking people to join it risked being labeled as a rabble-rouser and a subversive. Being a woman only complicated matters. Baker faced derision from those within the African-American community who believed women should keep out of political matters.

Baker shook off those who urged her to travel less, saying, "We must have the 'nerve' to take the Association to people wherever they are." On a typical day, she spent her mornings "visiting barber shops, filling stations, grocery stores and housewives," and her afternoons and evenings in the local "pool-rooms, boot black parlors, bars and grilles." She took her time with people, asking them questions about their families, their jobs, and their problems, not just for small talk's sake but because she was interested in their answers. She spent hours with the women of communities, making connections and building infrastructure. Even her speeches to gatherings of larger groups were made from her heart and spoken to the people. One of her coworkers remembered Baker as "a powerful speaker who talked without notes from her heart to the hearts of her audience. . . . Her speeches weren't full of statistics, nor were they anecdotal. They were to the point . . . very human and warm." Being a successful secretary, Baker said, "depended on both your disposition and your capacity to sort of stimulate people—and how you carried yourself, in terms of not being above people. . . . If you . . . somehow talk down to people, they can sense it. They can feel it. And they know whether you are talking *with* them, or talking *at* them, or talking *about* them."

Baker called upon many of the contacts she had made during her national tour with YNCL and her work with the WPA's Worker's Education Project. She was successful, but her achievements came at a cost. She worked long, wearying days, brushing off friends who begged her to slow down or take some time off. She also encountered opposition from those who did not appreciate her plainspoken, straightforward ways.

In the fall of 1941, Baker helped organize a membership campaign in Baltimore, Maryland, which raised over $5,000 and enrolled 4,000 new members. But the president of that branch, Lillie Jackson, complained in a letter to Walter White that Baker was disrespectful and difficult to get along with. White was unmoved by her complaint, since Jackson was known as a difficult person to get along with herself, but the conflict pointed out Baker's inability to kowtow to authority figures and her unwillingness to be swayed by impressive titles or résumés.

The branch chairman of a Richmond, Virginia, campaign said of Baker, "One of the most important and wonderful things that has happened to Richmond was the presence of the national field worker, Miss Ella J. Baker. . . . Never during her stay in Richmond did she slacken the pace. She was going from the time of her arrival until the time she left. . . . She has demonstrated to the people of Richmond and over the State of Virginia one characteristic very few people have and that is the wonderful and outstanding quality of mixing with any group of people and trying to help solve their problems."

In 1943, Baker was promoted to director of branches for the NAACP. She was responsible for supervising the field secretaries, and managing and coordinating the activities of all branches across the United States. The NAACP was in the midst of a huge membership surge, which made Baker's new role particularly influential. Between 1940 and 1946, the NAACP's ranks would swell from 40,000 to more than 450,000.

Baker wanted to empower the branches to go beyond

A group portrait of the thirty-second annual meeting of the NAACP in 1941. Among the attendees are Ella Baker and Roy Wilkins. *(Library of Congress)*

holding membership and fund-raising drives, and "hoping and waiting for the effects of national [NAACP legislative and legal] victories to trickle down to the South." She wanted to help them organize and fight their own battles on the local level.

One of Baker's first acts was to obtain the national leadership's approval to allow her to develop training programs for branch leaders so they might organize effective grassroots campaigns. Baker conducted ten conferences across the country between 1944 and 1946 with program titles such as "Techniques and Strategies of Minority Group Action," "Developing a Program of Action through Branch Committees," and "Postwar Problems and NAACP Branches." She challenged the branch leaders to ask themselves, "What are the things taking place in our community which we should like to see changed? What one thing can we be relatively certain we will be able to accomplish in a certain period of time?" She urged branch leaders to "take that one thing—getting a new school building; registering people to vote; getting bus transportation—take that one thing and work on it and get it done." For example, in Newton, Kansas, "that one thing" might be to end discrimination at lunch counters; in Council Bluffs, Iowa, it might be to end theater segregation; and in Farmville, Alabama, it might be to fight for higher salaries for African-American teachers.

As Baker worked to mobilize the people, the Second Great Migration was proceeding. From about 1941 to 1946, more than 1.5 million African Americans moved north to fill the record numbers of new jobs in the war-related manufacturing industries—jobs that were more accessible as a result of President Roosevelt's Executive Order 8802.

World War II began in Europe in 1939. Many Americans, still feeling the losses of the First World War, wanted to remain neutral in what they saw as a European conflict. But when the Japanese launched a surprise attack on the American Pacific fleet at Pearl Harbor on December 7, 1941, President Roosevelt asked Congress for a declaration of war.

Among those who volunteered to fight were thousands of African Americans. The army was still segregated, however, and many black leaders argued that it was absurd for American soldiers to fight Adolf Hitler's racism abroad when they were second-class citizens at home. A. Philip Randolph led a delegation to Washing-

A color guard of African-American soldiers at Fort Belvoir, Virginia, during World War II. *(Library of Congress)*

ton to plead with the president to desegregate the armed forces. Meanwhile, African-American enlistees were being turned away because the units reserved for them were full. Those who made it into service endured subpar conditions and all-white officer staffs, and were relegated to menial tasks. In 1944, at the Battle of the Bulge, General Dwight D. Eisenhower would desegregate the front lines temporarily when 2,000 black soldiers answered his call for volunteers to fight. The famous Tuskegee Airmen also saw combat action.

Black soldiers who served overseas experienced respectful, courteous treatment from whites for the first time. "The French had a certain kind of openness and warmth that they exhibited towards minorities that was just unexplainable. You wouldn't know you were black when you were in their company," said one African-American soldier. Another said, "We thought [Jim Crow] was the way it was supposed to be. We was dumb to the facts and didn't know. It opened up my eyes to the racial problems."

Many of these soldiers chose not to return to the Jim Crow South but to settle in northern cities. Racism and segregated neighborhoods were still prevalent there, but segregation in public facilities, transportation, restaurants, and bathrooms was not legislated. It was also easier to register to vote in the North.

The vote of African Americans strongly influenced Roosevelt's victories in eight states in the 1944 election. Two dozen African Americans entered state legislatures in the 1946 elections, and one was elected to the House of Representatives. During the 1950s, 1.5 million more African Americans would migrate north.

Contributing to the African-American voice in politics was the 1944 Supreme Court decision *Smith v. Allwright*. Lonnie E. Smith filed suit against S. S. Allwright, the white election official who refused to let him vote in the 1940 Texas primary because the law restricted primaries to white voters only. The Democratic Party argued the restriction was legal because it was a private organization and thus could control who participated in its meetings. William Hastie and Thurgood

Ella Baker in 1945 while working for the NAACP. *(Library of Congress)*

Marshall argued the case before the Supreme Court, earning a decision reading in part, "The right to vote in a primary for the nomination of candidates without discrimination by the State . . . is a right secured by the constitution."

Even as victories were achieved, there were still tensions in the hierarchy of the NAACP. Baker's focus on developing grassroots leadership for direct action campaigns had put her at odds with Walter White and other members of the NAACP's leadership team. These men were concerned that the direct action campaigns would anger whites to such an extent that the NAACP's legislative and legal strategy would be hindered. The NAACP was beginning to be challenged by some who felt its focus on working within the system and its top-down structure did not reflect the needs of the people it was supposed to represent.

In May 1946, Baker resigned from the NAACP, frustrated that her efforts were not fully appreciated. She had long been critical of Walter White's leadership style—sentiments that were widely shared in the NAACP headquarters but rarely spoken. She had challenged him for years to make changes to the way the organization was structured, staffed, and operated. White resisted her at every turn, and finally Baker had enough. She was typically straightforward about her reasons for leaving: "I feel the Association is falling short of its present possibilities; that the full capacities of the staff have not been used; that there is little chance of mine being utilized in the immediate future. Neither one nor all of these reasons would induce me to resign if I felt that objective and honest discussion were possible and that remedial measures would follow."

Letters flowed in from around the country as news of Baker's resignation spread. One from an NAACP leader in Mobile, Alabama, read, "All of us here and people throughout the county whom we have talked to, and who know you, have nothing but praise [for your work] . . . we have grown to love you." Another came from G. F. Porter of the Dallas NAACP branch: "It made me sick to learn that you are going to leave us, for I feel so close to you and think you are an ideal woman for the position you are holding. I hope the National Office will be able to persuade you to stay."

Though she disagreed with its organizational philosophy, Baker still believed in the NAACP's ideals. "I shall keep faith with the basic principles of the NAACP and with the faith vested in it by the people," she wrote, and continued to travel and speak on the organization's behalf for several years.

The same year she left the NAACP, Baker took on an additional responsibility when she adopted her nine-year-old niece, Jackie, the daughter of her sister, Maggie, who had always been known as the irresponsible sibling. Ella's mother had cared for Jackie, but she was eighty years old and no longer able to keep up with the young girl. Jackie needed a home and Baker provided it. Jackie later said of her aunt's decision to take her in, "She thought that every child should have the opportunity to grow up with someone who loved them and someone who could care for them. And she felt she could give me that."

Of Baker's child-rearing style, Jackie said, "She was very firm, but she would never say you could not do something and that's it. She always thought you should have an explanation. You knew that the love was there and there wasn't anything she wouldn't do for you."

Baker raised Jackie according to the same community-based principles her own mother had instilled. Jackie remembered an example:

> On one occasion, I wanted sneakers. But I didn't really need them. I had shoes. There was a little boy next door who took a liking to my aunt. He was beginning to play basketball with the other boys. He had no shoes at all and he wanted sneakers, too. So we decided we would buy him sneakers, and I could wait for another time to buy sneakers for me. We decided on that because Aunt Ella felt that his self-image had been destroyed because he did not have the proper attire to play in. And we could sacrifice my sneakers for his at this point if it helped him in any way. If he began to feel good about himself, then it was worth it. That was the type of thing she would do for people.

Baker was forty-two when she took in Jackie. Though she cut back her travel schedule to be with Jackie as much as she could, she did not give up her work and instead relied on her husband and a neighbor for help. As always, she patched together employment in paid and unpaid positions, giving all she could to help the causes she believed in: the American Cancer Society, the New York Urban League, the National Association of Consumers, and the Consumer Advisory Committee of the President's Council of Economic Advisors.

One cause that was especially important to Baker was the Journey of Reconciliation. The plan was for an interracial group of activists to travel by bus on a two-week trip through Virginia, North Carolina, Tennessee, and Kentucky to test the 1946 *Morgan v. Virginia* Supreme Court decision. The case took its name from the plaintiff, Irene Morgan, who had boarded a Greyhound bus in Gloucester, Virginia, in 1944, headed for Baltimore, Maryland. Morgan, who was recovering from a miscarriage, took a seat in the back of the bus in the area segregated for African-American passengers. Her seat mate was a young mother carrying her baby. A few miles into the trip, a young white couple boarded the bus. All the seating in the white section was taken, so the bus driver ordered Morgan and the young mother to move. Morgan refused. It took an armed sheriff to bodily drag her from the bus. She was arrested and taken to jail. Morgan's case made it all the way to the Supreme Court, where it was argued by NAACP's Thurgood Marshall. The court's 6-1 decision struck down Virginia's segregated seating laws on buses traveling from one state to another. Despite the ruling, however, de facto segregation continued on many interstate buses.

Ella Baker and Bayard Rustin were two of the coordinators for the Journey of Reconciliation, which was cosponsored by the Fellowship of Reconciliation (FOR) and the Congress of Racial Equality (CORE). FOR was an international, interfaith organization founded to fight for world peace and an end to poverty, violence, bigotry, and racism. CORE was an interracial organization founded to pioneer nonviolent direct action campaigns to fight discrimination. Bayard Rustin was an African-American Quaker, a member of the Young Communist

Baker's friend and colleague, Bayard Rustin. *(A. Philip Randolph Institute)*

League during the Depression, a field secretary for FOR, and a member of CORE. He was also homosexual. His Communist affiliations and homosexual orientation would force him to keep a low public profile throughout the civil rights movement, although his behind-the-scenes work would be indispensable to the movement's success.

Baker had every intention of participating in the actual ride, but the men in the group refused to allow women to join them. They argued that it was far too dangerous. In April 1947, sixteen men—eight African Americans and eight whites—set out to integrate buses.

Members of the 1947 Journey of Reconciliation. *Left to right:* Worth Randle, Wallace Nelson, Ernest Bromley, James Peck, Igal Roodenko, Bayard Rustin, Joseph Felmet, George Houser, and Andrew Johnson. *(Bayard Rustin Estate)*

Whites sat in the back and African Americans sat in the front. Police officers in Chapel Hill, North Carolina, stopped the bus and arrested four of the riders—two whites and two African Americans—and charged them with violating North Carolina's segregated bus seating laws.

Judge Henry Whitfield presided over the court hearing. With absolute disregard for the Supreme Court's *Morgan* decision, Judge Henry Whitfield found the four riders guilty of breaking Jim Crow laws. He sentenced the African Americans, including Bayard Rustin, to thirty days hard labor on a chain gang. He sentenced the two white men, Igal Roodenko and Joseph Felmet, even more harshly, saying: "It's about time you Jews from New York learned that you can't come down here bringing your niggers with you to upset the customs of the South. Just to teach you a lesson, I gave your black boys thirty days, and I give you ninety."

A total of twelve men were arrested during the two-week ride. They had been carefully schooled in the tenants of nonviolent resistance. The riders faced both opposition and support from across racial lines—some African Americans pleaded with them to obey bus drivers who asked them to move, while some white passengers spoke out in support of their stance. But in the end, the journey was little more than a symbolic gesture.

As America neared the midpoint of the twentieth century, the specter of Jim Crow still hung heavy on the South. World War II underscored the inherent inequality of segregation. Black soldiers fought to stop Hitler's racism, then returned to face discrimination at home. Baker pointed out this hypocrisy: "America cannot hope to lead the peoples of the world to freedom, justice and equality without achieving for all of its own citizens a full measure of these virtues. Hence, the fate of the minority groups in America is bound with the fate of the peoples of the world; and the prevalence of human freedom and peace throughout the world will be conditioned by the extent to which democracy and freedom is enjoyed by all Americans regardless of race, creed or color."

President Roosevelt had not lived to see the end of

Roosevelt's successor, President Harry S. Truman.

the war. He was succeeded in office by his vice president, Harry Truman. Truman came under pressure from A. Philip Randolph and other leaders. In 1947, he appointed a fifteen-man president's commission on civil rights to examine racism in America. The commission issued its recommendations in an October 1947 report, which was called "To Secure These Rights." It called for immediate intervention by the federal government to protect the rights of all its citizens and enforce the existing statutes granting those rights.

On July 26, 1948, President Truman signed two Executive Orders—one creating a Fair Employment Board to eliminate racial discrimination in the federal government's hiring practices and another to establish the president's committee on equality of treatment and opportunity in the armed services, which finally ended segregation in the armed services.

Baker was heartened by Truman's actions and continued her efforts on behalf of the NAACP. In 1952, at the age of forty-eight, she became the first woman president of the New York City branch. Baker moved the branch office from downtown New York to Harlem and ran it the way she had wanted the branches to operate when she was director of branches some nine years before.

The local issue she chose to focus on was education, specifically the tracking system used in New York City's public schools. Tracking systems sorted out students according to their assessed potential. Some were sent to college preparatory classes, others on a path to trade school, and some just moved through toward graduation. Opponents of the system argued it segregated African-American students and barred them from a college education. Baker organized parent groups and wrote letters to the mayor and the school superintendent. Baker held mass meetings to educate parents and forged an alliance with the significant Puerto Rican population, whose children were also treated unfairly. Thus, when the Supreme Court issued its *Brown v. Board of Education* decision in 1954, Baker believed it would be the catalyst that would end the kind of racial discrimination she had been fighting in New York City's public schools.

Five

Legislative Victories

Brown v. Board of Education overturned the fifty-eight-year-old *Plessy v. Ferguson* decision by challenging the constitutionality of racial segregation in public schools. NAACP attorneys Thurgood Marshall, George E. Hayes, and James Nabrit Jr. argued the case. They borrowed portions of Pauli Murray's final Howard Law School project to support their arguments. Murray had argued that *Plessy v. Ferguson* should be overturned because segregation was a violation of the Fourteenth Amendment's equal protection clause on two grounds: classification on the basis of race was subjective and the psychological injury caused by the "separate but equal" doctrine "place[d] the Negro in an inferior social and legal position," and "[did] violence to the personality of the individual affected, whether he [wa]s white or black."

May 17, 1954

Supreme Court of the United States
Washington, D.C.

Dear Chief:

This is a day that will live in glory. It is also a great day in the history of the Court, and not in the least for the course of deliberation which brought about the result. I congratulate you.

Very sincerely,
Felix Frankfurter

A note sent from Justice Felix Frankfurter to Chief Justice Warren on the day the Supreme Court issued its 9-0 decision in *Brown v. Board of Education. (Library of Congress)*

In 1954, the nine justices of the court unanimously agreed.

Chief Justice Earl Warren explained the court's opinion that to separate African-American students from white students "of similar age and qualifications solely because of their race generates a feeling of inferiority as to their status in the community that may affect their hearts and minds in a way unlikely to be undone."

Southern white segregationists' reaction to the decision was open defiance. Georgia's Governor Herman Talmadge said, "The United States Supreme Court by its decision has reduced the Constitution to a mere scrap of paper . . . The People of Georgia believe in, adhere to and will fight for their right under the United States and Georgia constitutions to manage their own affairs. They cannot and will not accept a bald political decree without basis in law or practicality which overturns their accepted pattern of life." The Jackson *Daily News* in Mississippi supported the elected officials who vowed never to implement the decision, editorializing, "Even though it was delivered by a unanimous vote of the nine members of the nation's highest tribunal, Mississippi cannot and will not try to abide by such a decision." The paper went on to describe the decision as "the worst thing that has happened to the South since carpetbaggers and scalawags took charge of our civil government in reconstruction days." Southerners referred to day of the *Brown v. Board of Education* decision as "Black Monday."

Within two months of the decision, White Citizens' Councils were formed to fight the Supreme Court's decision and any other efforts to integrate southern society. By 1956, there were nearly 80,000 members in hundreds of chapters across the South. They were nicknamed the "uptown Ku Klux Klans" because they consisted of mostly middle- to upper-class white businessmen and politicians, and used economic reprisals instead of

A White Citizens' Council bumper sticker from the 1950s.

violence to ensure the continuance of segregation. Many state governments sponsored council films that featured the benefits of segregation. The Mississippi state legislature formed a State Sovereignty Commission which contributed funds to secret networks that were authorized to root out African American or white citizens who worked for desegregation.

In March 1956, eighty-one southern congressmen and nineteen southern senators signed the "Southern Manifesto," which condemned the *Brown v. Board of Education* decision, claiming it violated states' rights and subverted the Constitution of the United States.

The Jim Crow conditions under which African Americans lived in the South received further nationwide attention with the murder of fourteen-year-old Emmett Till. Emmett Till was from Chicago and visiting relatives

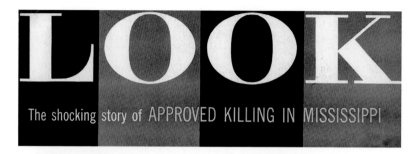

The shocking story of APPROVED KILLING IN MISSISSIPPI

A headline from the cover of the January 1956 *Look* magazine issue in which Emmett Till's murderers admitted to their crime. *(Library of Congress)*

who lived near Money, Mississippi, in Tallahatchie County, where he was accused of whistling at a white woman. He was kidnapped and murdered for it. His stripped body was found floating along the banks of the Mississippi River four days later. A seventy-five-pound cotton-gin fan was tied to his neck with barbed wire.

Photographs of Till's disfigured body in an open casket were distributed nationwide. News that an all-white jury found the killers not guilty roused anger throughout the country. The killers later confessed to the murder in a story published in *Look* magazine. Medgar Evers was the NAACP field officer in Jackson, Mississippi, at the time of Emmett Till's murder. He urged the NAACP to get involved. Evers's reasons for joining the NAACP were rooted, in part, in his experiences as a child growing up in Decatur, Mississippi:

> When I was eleven or twelve a close friend of the family got lynched... because he sassed back a white woman. They just left him dead on the ground. Everyone in town knew it but never [said] a word in

Civil rights activist Medgar Evers. *(Library of Congress)*

public. I went down and saw his bloody clothes. They left those clothes on a fence for about a year. Every Negro in town was supposed to get the message from those clothes and I can see those clothes now in my mind's eye . . . But nothing was said in public. No sermons in church. No news. No protest. It was as though this man just dissolved except for the bloody clothes. . . . Just before I went into the Army I began wondering how long I could stand it. I used to watch the Saturday night sport of white men trying to run down a Negro with their car, or white gangs coming through town to beat up a Negro.

Following a stint in the army during World War II,

Evers tried to enroll in the University of Mississippi's law school to test the *Brown v. Board of Education* decision. He fought the university's various stalling tactics for some time before he gave up and decided to dedicate himself to working for the NAACP. At the time of Till's murder, Evers was investigating crimes against African Americans that the FBI refused to pursue.

Within the civil rights movement, Till's murder became emblematic of the frustration some workers felt with the NAACP's legalistic agenda. While they knew that working within the system would lead to important gains, they chafed at watching gross miscarriages of justice go unchallenged. But many at the NAACP headquarters felt Mississippi was a hopeless cause and wanted to focus their efforts in places with more potential for change. This led to the formation of several smaller organizations, often led by local ministers or women's groups, which took direct action, usually in the form of protests. This triggered a divide in the movement that sometimes created tension between older and newer organizations. Walter Williams, Roy Wilkins, and other leaders of the NAACP were sometimes uncomfortable with this groundswell, but it was impossible to hold back.

The first of these local actions to draw national attention was the Montgomery bus boycott. The Women's Political Council of Montgomery, Alabama, had long looked for a way to protest the daily humiliations African Americans suffered on the city's segregated public

This famous photograph shows Rosa Parks during her sit-in protest on a bus in Montgomery, Alabama. *(Library of Congress)*

buses. On December 1, 1955, NAACP worker Rosa Parks was arrested for refusing to cede her seat to a white man. As soon as they heard the news, JoAnn Robinson, a professor at the all-black Alabama State College and president of the Women's Political Council, and E. D. Nixon, the president of the Montgomery chapter of the NAACP, decided that Parks's arrest might be the event around which such a protest could be rallied. Robinson mimeographed thousands of fliers announcing a bus boycott and had them distributed by students, political council members, and members of the various women's groups in the churches of Montgomery.

The Montgomery Improvement Association (MIA), headed by the young minister Martin Luther King Jr., was organized to support the boycott. With the MIA's

A picture from the early days of the Highlander Folk School in Monteagle, Tennessee.

help, the majority of Montgomery's black citizens refused to ride the city's buses for more than a year. Their courageous act garnered national attention and was finally resolved when the Supreme Court ruled that segregated seating on buses was in violation of the Fourteenth Amendment. As opposed to the *Morgan* decision, this one affected intrastate buses, not interstate.

Rosa Parks had been emboldened to stand her ground in part because of her attendance at a weeklong session held at the Highlander Folk School earlier that year. The Highlander Folk School was founded in Monteagle, Tennessee, by Myles Horton, a poor white sharecropper's son, as a place were people could attend interracial workshops to learn how to foster social change. Baker supported Highlander because its emphasized reaching out to people larger organizations often ignored—the poor and the illiterate.

Ella Baker and Rosa Parks had been friends since they first met in 1946, when Baker was traveling for the NAACP. Baker had conducted one of the workshops that Rosa Parks attended during her time at Highlander in the summer of 1955. Parks said of her weeklong Highlander experience, "We forgot about what color anybody was. I was forty-two years old, and it was one of the few times in my life up to that point when I did not feel any hostility from white people. I experienced people of different races and backgrounds meeting together in workshops and living together in peace and harmony."

Ella Baker, Stanley Levison, A. Philip Randolph, and Bayard Rustin formed a group they called In Friendship, a coalition of northern business, political, labor, and religious groups interested in raising money to support the Montgomery bus boycott and to support efforts to implement the *Brown v. Board of Education* decision. Baker served as executive secretary of In Friendship until it dissolved in 1959.

Through the work of In Friendship, Stanley Levison, a longtime member of the American Jewish Congress, lawyer, businessman, and former socialist, and Bayard Rustin moved into Martin Luther King Jr.'s inner circle of close confidantes. Baker didn't get as close to King as they did. As she explained it, "After all, who was I? I was female, I was old. I didn't have any PhD." Further-more, she was not one to shy away from asking questions or taking an opposing view. "I did not just subscribe to a theory just because it came out of the mouth of the leader," she said.

The Montgomery bus boycott proved that grass roots action could work. It was a turning point in the civil rights movement. Ella Baker summed it up as an event in which "thousands of individuals, just black ordinary people, subjected themselves to inconveniences that were certainly beyond the thinking of most folk . . . [creating] a momentum that had not been seen, even in the work of the NAACP. And it was something that suggested the potential for widespread action through-out the South."

Six

Going South

In January 1957, Ella Baker and Bayard Rustin headed south. They joined more than sixty ministers and other civic organization leaders from almost a dozen southern states in Atlanta, Georgia, for a meeting at the Ebenezer Baptist Church. Their purpose was to make a national movement out of the Montgomery bus boycott momentum. Two of the more prominent ministers attending this meeting were Martin Luther King Jr. and Reverend Ralph Abernathy, the pastor of the First Baptist Church in Montgomery and a close friend of King's.

After much discussion, the group decided to form the Southern Christian Leadership Conference (SCLC) as an "organization of organizations," instead of an organization of individual members. Instead of joining the SCLC, one would join one of its member organizations.

The objective was to be a southern-based group to complement the northern-based NAACP and to be the "political arm of the black church." They formalized the organization a month later at a meeting in New Orleans.

The SCLC's objectives would be to use nonviolent methods to conduct direct action campaigns to end segregation in public facilities and to register two million African-American voters before the 1960 election. To emphasize its nonviolent stance, the SCLC leadership adopted as its motto: "Not one hair of one head of one white person shall be harmed."

The SCLC organizers wanted to minimize the potential for conflict with the NAACP, now headed by Roy Wilkins. He had assumed the position of executive director upon the death of Walter White in 1955 and continued the NAACP's focus on the legislative and legal arenas. Despite the SCLC's attempt to not rile the older organization, Roy Wilkins and others worried that direct action campaigns would undermine the NAACP's efforts.

Martin Luther King Jr. was elected president of the SCLC, and Ralph Abernathy was appointed secretary-treasurer. Neither Rosa Parks, JoAnn Robinson, nor any other women instrumental in the success of the Montgomery Bus Boycott were invited to sit on the SCLC's board of directors. Neither was Ella Baker, who had been instrumental in the organization's formation. Though the civil rights movement existed to fight discrimination, its focus was on race. Women were consistently

Dr. Martin Luther King Jr. *(Library of Congress)*

discounted. This was a conflict that would continue for years to come.

Nonetheless, Baker continued to work diligently in the movement. The SCLC's first national exposure occurred with the Prayer Pilgrimage for Freedom, held at the Lincoln Memorial in Washington, D.C., on May 17, 1957, to commemorate the third anniversary of *Brown v. Board of Education* and to garner support for the Civil Rights Act of 1957. Baker and Rustin were the two organizers of the event, and one of their challenges was to distance the pilgrimage from allegations of Communist ties. Communism was associated with the United States' great Cold War enemy, the Soviet Union, and anyone with Communist leaning was swiftly branded as anti-American. Baker and Rustin described the Prayer Pilgrimage as "a spiritual assembly, primarily by the Negro clergy, and the NAACP. In such an assembly, there will be no place for the irreligious. . . . No communists have been or will be invited to participate in the program either as a speaker, singer, prayer leader, or scripture leader. . . . The Official Call, issued on April 5, 1957, invites all who love justice and dignity and liberty, who love their country, to join in a Prayer Pilgrimage to Washington on May 17, 1957."

The SCLC's Prayer Pilgrimage was attended by nearly 30,000 people and seemed to achieve its goal of gaining support for the proposed Civil Rights Act of 1957. President Dwight D. Eisenhower, who had previously been of the opinion that legislating civil rights could not work until the hearts and minds of Americans were changed, authorized his vice president, Richard Nixon, to meet with civil rights leaders to discuss the pending bill. MIA, CORE, SCLC, and NAACP representatives

On the stage at the Prayer Pilgrimage on May 17, 1957. *From left to right:* Roy Wilkins *(in light suit),* A. Philip Randolph, Thomas Kilgore, Martin Luther King Jr. *(Library of Congress)*

were all on hand to meet with the vice president to voice their support for its passage.

The Civil Rights Act of 1957 signified the first civil rights legislation passed by Congress since Reconstruction. It met with strong resistance from southern senators. In 1948, Strom Thurmond of South Carolina had reassured his white constituents "there's not enough troops in the army to force the southern people to break down segregation and admit the nigger race into our theaters, into our swimming pools, into our homes, and into our churches."

The Civil Rights Act had the backing of Senate majority leader Lyndon B. Johnson, a Democrat from Texas.

Under his watch, the act was eventually passed, though many concessions were made. The diluted version of the bill encouraged African Americans to register to vote but did nothing to penalize anyone obstructing their efforts. Many black leaders thought the bill was so weak as to be almost pointless. Others, including Bayard Rustin and Ella Baker, saw it as a symbolic victory. Either way, it was clear the issue would have to be revisited in the years to come.

It was proving difficult to get local school districts to comply with the *Brown v. Board of Education* decision. The situation exploded onto the national scene again on September 4, 1957, when nine African-American students tried to register for school at Little Rock Central High in Little Rock, Arkansas, after a federal court ordered Little Rock to comply with *Brown v. Board of Education.* Governor Orval Faubus refused to comply with the federal court's order and directed the Arkansas National Guard to surround the school to keep the student from enrolling.

Governor Faubus ordered the schools closed at the start of the 1958 school year. Days later, the Supreme Court issued its *Cooper v. Aaron* decision, which declared that state officials must comply with the court's order to desegregate schools. Faubus attempted, instead, to lease Little Rock's school buildings to private entities to be run as whites-only schools. A June 1959 federal court ruled the governor's attempt unconstitutional, and Faubus was forced to reopen Little Rock's schools in September 1959.

The nine students involved in the school integration case in Little Rock, Arkansas, with civil rights activist Daisy Bates *(standing second from right)*, who coordinated the integration effort. *(Library of Congress)*

One of the ways white segregationists maintained power was by keeping African Americans from voting— only 22 percent of African-American citizens were registered. Those who did try to vote encountered poll taxes, literacy tests, and the threat of violence designed to keep them from the polls. The SCLC's leadership decided to launch a massive voter registration drive in an effort to double the numbers of African- American voters and to "challenge blacks to take on the responsibilities of fighting for their rights." They called it the Crusade for Citizenship and targeted a kickoff date of February 12, 1958, the anniversary of President Lincoln's birthday.

With no SCLC staff in place to coordinate the voter registration drive, Ella Baker was invited, at the insistence of Rustin and Levison, to become the SCLC's interim executive director. She was fifty-four years old and later said wryly of her hire, "Someone [had] to run the mimeographing machine."

Rustin and Levison knew that Baker was the best person for the job of organizing a massive movement across the South due to the contacts she had developed during her years with the NAACP, YNCL, and WPA. Baker agreed to accept the job. She had been separated from her husband on and off for years (their divorce would become final in 1958), and her niece, Jackie, was nineteen and on her own. She was now free to direct all her energy to civil rights.

Though she kept her New York apartment, Baker moved to Atlanta in mid-January 1958, where she was alarmed to discover just how poor the SCLC was: "I had to function out of a telephone booth and my pocketbook. Nobody had made any provisions for space, hadn't even thought about it." With less than four weeks until the February 12 kickoff of the voter registration drive, Baker dove into preparations. She wrote and submitted press releases to dozens of newspapers, and she wrote and distributed letters and flyers to hundreds of church leaders, women's groups, civic organizations, and citizens. She spent hours on the telephone, making calls to local leaders to solicit their support and to line up speakers for all twenty-two rallies.

The city of Atlanta around the time Baker moved there in the late 1950s. *(Library of Congress)*

The SCLC's Crusade for Citizenship kickoff was not very successful. Less than four weeks was not enough time to adequately prepare. There was not enough money to get the word out. Baker was the only staff member. Further contributing to the Crusade kickoff's dismal performance was the fact that many SCLC members were also members of the NAACP and had been encouraged by the latter not to fully cooperate. The NAACP feared losing its position as the most important civil rights organization. Nonetheless, the SCLC did not want to abandon its objective of doubling the numbers of registered African-American voters and pressed ahead.

The SCLC leadership began looking for a permanent executive director. Baker had understood that her position was only temporary and supported their decision to bring Reverend John Tilly on board in May 1958. Baker admitted she "knew from the beginning that having a woman be an executive of SCLC was not something that would go over with the male-dominated leadership. And then, of course, my personality wasn't right . . . I was not afraid to disagree with the higher authorities." She added, "You see . . . it was more important to go ahead. I may as well play the supporting role there as anywhere else. So I stayed on." Baker spent the next several months traveling across the South teaching local community leaders how to conduct voter registration campaigns and fund-raising events.

However, Reverend Tilly was fired less than a year later, in 1959, and Baker was brought back in as interim director. She urged the leadership to concentrate on finding and training local leaders to coordinate community-based direct action campaigns. She wanted the SCLC to function as a "group-centered leadership [organization], rather than a leadership-centered group." She said, "We are really passing though a revolutionary period. . . . SCLC has a real opportunity to develop the mass action that we must have to implement school decisions, the 1957 Civil Rights Act, etc. But if we fail to act, sooner or later some other group will provide the leadership, because mass action is sorely needed."

Baker described her objective in her "SCLC as a Crusade" memo. She wrote, "The word *crusade* connotes for me a vigorous movement with high purpose and involving masses of people." She continued, "It is possible to contact four persons an hour; and in eight hours a month, one minister could reach 30 persons, at least. If one thousand [ministers] gave 8 hours it would mean 30,000 persons in one month. For 10 months this could mean 300,000 persons. If initiated and accepted by the leadership of SCLC it is quite possible, I believe, to commit 1,000 leaders to give eight hours a month to work directly with the people." In this manner, Baker concluded, efforts like voter registration "could take on crusading proportions."

Some four months later, Baker found the crusade she'd been looking for.

Seven

SNCC

On February 1, 1960, four North Carolina Agricul-tural and Technical College freshman students (Ezell Blair Jr., Franklin McCain, Joseph McNeil, and David Richmond) decided to challenge North Carolina's seg-regated seating laws by sitting at the whites-only lunch counter in the F. W. Woolworth store in Greensboro, North Carolina. The students were told by the waitress, "I'm sorry. We don't serve coloreds in here." Having just purchased school supplies at a register no more than two feet from the lunch counter, Ezell Blair Jr. responded respectfully, "I beg to disagree with you." The four students sat at the lunch counter until the store closed.

The next day, twenty of their fellow students joined them at the counter, and on the third day, students occupied sixty-three of the lunch counter's sixty-six

North Carolina A&T College students during the 1960 sit-in at the Woolworth lunch counter in downtown Greensboro. *(Library of Congress)*

seats. Within a week, sit-ins were taking place in Durham and Winston-Salem, North Carolina, followed by sit-ins in Charlotte, Raleigh, Fayetteville, and Elizabeth City. The movement continued to spread, and two months later, student sit-ins had taken place in more than fifty cities across nine southern states. In March, the students conducting sit-in protests in Atlanta posted their "Appeal for Human Rights" in a paid advertisement in the *Atlanta Constitution*. It read, in part:

> We do not intend to wait placidly for those rights which are already legally and morally ours to be meted out to us one at a time. Today's youth will not sit by submissively, while being denied all of the rights, privileges, and joys of life. We want to state clearly and unequivocally that we cannot tolerate, in a nation professing democracy and among people professing Christianity, the discriminatory conditions

which the Negro is living today in Atlanta, Georgia—supposedly one of the most progressive cities in the South.

The initial Woolworth counter sit-in and the way it inspired other students captivated Baker. Since the end of the Montgomery boycott, much of the black leadership, including Martin Luther King Jr., had been at a loss as to how to proceed. The sit-ins showed that aggressive nonviolence was possible—that people did not need to

CIVIL DISOBEDIENCE

Inspired by the American writer Henry David Thoreau (1817-1862), Indian leader Mohandas Karamchand Gandhi popularized the notion of civil disobedience during his country's struggle for independence from Great Britain. American civil rights leaders, including Bayard Rustin, traveled to India to study civil disobedience and bring the practice back to the United States. Operating under the theory that one could refuse to obey or uphold an unjust law, practitioners used nonviolent protest to resist without causing injury or damage. Peaceful protest has since been used by movements around the world, from the sit-ins of the civil rights movement to the fight against apartheid in Africa. Most demonstrators still follow the principles of resistance outlined by Gandhi in 1921:

1. A satyagrahi, i.e., a civil resister, will harbor no anger.

2. He will suffer the anger of the opponent.

3. In so doing he will put up with assaults from the opponent, never retaliate; but he will not submit, out of fear of punishment or the like, to any order given in anger.

4. When any person in authority seeks to arrest a civil resister, he will voluntarily submit to the arrest, and he will not resist the attachment or removal of his own property, if any, when it is sought to be confiscated by authorities.

5. If a civil resister has any property in his possession as a trustee, he will refuse to surrender it, even though in defending it he might lose his life. He will, however, never retaliate.

6. Not retaliating includes not swearing and not cursing.

7. Therefore a civil resister will never insult his opponent, and therefore also not take part in many of the newly coined cries that are contrary to the spirit of ahimsa.

8. A civil resister will not salute the Union Jack, nor will he insult it or officials, English or Indian.

9. In the course of the struggle, if anyone insults an official or commits an assault upon him, a civil resister will protect such official or officials from the insult or attack even at the risk of his life.

wait to be victimized before they could protest. Baker saw the sit-ins as the spark the civil rights movement needed—they were representative of the desires of the people and they were localized, direct-action, non-violent confrontations.

Baker asked the SCLC for $800 to hold a Highlander-style conference at Shaw University for students during their spring break in April 1960. She called it the "Southwide Student Leadership Conference on Nonviolent Resistance to Segregation." Her objective

was to see how the student sit-ins might be better organized and coordinated. "It was very obvious . . . that there
was little or no communication between those who sat
in, say Charlotte, North Carolina, and those who sat in
at some other place in Virginia or Alabama. They were
motivated by what the North Carolina four had started,
but they were not in contact with each other . . . you
couldn't build a sustaining force just based on sponta-
neity," said Baker.

Close to two hundred white and African-American
students showed up, plus adult representatives of the
various civil rights organizations; the latter were vying
to take over what appeared to be a promising student
movement. The SCLC was one such organization and
believed their chances of success were greater than
those of the NAACP or CORE, for example, because as
Baker later explained, "The Southern Christian Leadership Conference felt that they could influence how
things went [with the students]. They were interested in
having the students become an arm of SCLC. They were
most confident that this would be their baby, because I
called the meeting. . . . Well, I disagreed. I wasn't one to
say yes because it came from the Reverend King. So
when it was proposed that [SCLC] could influence . . .
what [the students] wanted done, I was outraged. I
walked out."

With Baker's help, the students managed to avoid an
affiliation with any one of the existing civil rights
organizations and instead formed their own, which they

A pin displaying the Student Nonviolent Coordinating Committee logo.

called the Student Nonviolent Coordinating Committee (SNCC), pronounced "snick." Baker said, "Most of the youngsters had been trained . . . to follow adults . . . . I felt they ought to have a chance to learn to think things through and to make the decisions." One SNCC member, Judy Richardson, said, "What was nice about Miss Baker is you never felt that she had a personal agenda that she was trying to put on. It was always about what is good for the organization, for black people, for whatever the larger issue was. [With] other adults you never really knew what else was hidden . . . what else they were trying to get through that they weren't talking about." Baker concurred:

> The chief emphasis I tried to make was their right to
> make their own decision. . . . The only reason that I
> became relevant . . . was because I had lived through

certain experiences and had had certain opportunities to gather information and organizational experience. . . . I have always felt that if there is any time in our existence that you have a right to make mistakes it should be when you're young, cause you have some time to live down some of the mistakes, or to offset them. I felt that what [the students] were doing was certainly . . . creative [and] much more productive than anything that had happened in my life, and it shouldn't be stifled. . . . I must have sensed also that it was useless to try to put the brakes on, because it was unleashed enthusiasm . . . an overflow of a dam that had been penned up for years, and it had to run its course.

Baker used her long-standing technique of helping people help themselves when working with the students by employing what they called her "little trick." She would sit back and quietly observe the group. When she noticed someone who seemed to have something to say, she would go sit by them and engage them in a side conversation to learn their thoughts on the subject. Baker would then call the group's attention to that person, declaring, "Look, here's somebody with something to say about that." She would also prod the group by asking questions: "I usually tried to present whatever participation I had in terms of questions, and tried to get people to reach certain decisions by questioning some of the things themselves."

Bob Moses came to SNCC near its very beginning with a master's in philosophy from Harvard and experience as a math teacher. He later said of Baker's role at SNCC:

> It was Ella more than anyone else who gave us the space to operate in. As long as she was sitting there in the meetings, no one else could dare come in and say I think you should do this or that, because no one could pull rank on her. Her stature was such that there wasn't anyone from the NAACP to Dr. King who could get by her. I think that the actual course of the SNCC movement is a testimony to the fact that the students were left free to develop on their own. That was her real contribution.

Baker had finally found the organization that was dedicated to doing what she wanted. It was a participant-run group that was respectful of all its members. In 1960, at the age of fifty-six, Baker resigned as SCLC's interim executive director and she became SNCC's advisor. She set up their office in Atlanta and earned her living working with Atlanta's YWCA as a human relations consultant to the National Student YWCA.

Representatives of CORE, the National College and Youth Branch of the NAACP, the SCLC, the National Student YWCA, and others were invited to send observers to SNCC meetings. Some had representatives who were also allowed to vote. From the beginning, women played an equal role in the organization thanks to Baker's example and the group's early irreverence for conventional organizational formats.

During a series of marathon sessions, some lasting twenty-four hours, SNCC adopted an organizational structure, a constitution, and a slogan. Baker helped the group implement a clear set of procedures and guidelines. She made sure the elected leaders would be directed by input from the group. Her experience with the top-down leadership of the NAACP and the SCLC had convinced her SNCC should be responsive to the people it served.

SNCC's constitution read, in part, "SNCC shall serve as a channel of coordination and communication for the student movement. By direction of its Executive Committee through its staff it shall have authority to initiate programs in areas where none presently exists, and to work closely with local protest groups in the intensification of the movement." Its slogan was, "We are all leaders."

SNCC spent its first several months coordinating sit-in activities and sponsoring student workshops on nonviolent resistance. The training paid off. News coverage captured images of well-dressed groups of African-American and white students sitting politely at lunch counters while having food and drinks poured over their heads, cigarettes burned into the back of their necks, and taunts screamed in their ears. Most absurdly, the students were usually the ones arrested—for violating Jim Crow laws.

Many of the arrested students adopted the "jail-no-bail" tactic and refused to pay fines or bail themselves out of jail. This placed pressure on local jails and captured the nation's consciousness. Ralph McGill of the *Atlanta Constitution* said of the sits-ins, "No argument in a court of law could have dramatized the immorality and irrationality of such a custom as did the sit-ins."

Within eighteen months, SNCC volunteers had organized sit-ins in over one hundred cities across the South, involving tens of thousands of demonstrators and resulting in several thousand arrests. Sit-ins electrified the student movement, demonstrated the power of direct action campaigns, and resulted in several chain stores ending segregation at their lunch counters.

There were problems, however. While the sit-ins were proceeding, SNCC's mass meetings were often deadlocked over what to do next. One faction wanted to focus on direct action campaigns; the other wanted to focus on voter registration. In the end, Ella Baker and James Forman, another SNCC cofounder, convinced the group they could do both. Forman was a teacher from Chicago who regularly visited his grandmother's farm in Mississippi and knew how difficult it was for African Americans to vote there. He had joined CORE earlier to provide relief services to Tennessee sharecroppers evicted for trying to register to vote. He had an interest in pushing voting campaigns.

Diane Nash, a student at Fisk University, was chosen to head up the direct action efforts. Charles Jones, a

SNCC member James Forman. *(AP Photo)*

Charlotte minister in his twenties, was chosen to head up the voter registration efforts. Baker was asked to serve as executive secretary of SNCC and to keep the overall organization on track. She declined the offer because she thought SNCC should remain a student-run organization, and James Forman was chosen instead. Baker later praised Forman as "the guy who made [SNCC] into an organization . . . a fighting force."

Baker continued in an advisory role, modeling by

example her long-held beliefs that every person had something to offer and that personal relationships were the key to engaging people. These beliefs became ingrained components of SNCC's student training. "There was no room for talking down to anyone," said Barbara Jones, a SNCC member. "There was never the expressed attitude that a person who was illiterate had something less to offer." Another SNCC member said, "We'd sit sometimes and rock on the porch for hours. Our intention was to finally convince a person to go and register. But we'd sit and we'd listen, and we'd listen to the person talk about survival and talk about families . . . I think some of the most important lessons I learned were on the porches of people who couldn't read or write their names." Bob Moses remembered, "Whenever you want to really do something with somebody else then the first thing you have to do is make this personal connection, you have to find out who it is you're really working with. You really have to be interested in that person to work with them. . . . You saw that all across the South in the grassroots and rural people. That was their style and Ella carried that style into this other level."

Baker believed that smaller, local changes that improved the lives of the participants in the short term would gradually become a powerful force in the national struggle. SNCC volunteer Jane Stembridge described the role SNCC volunteers were trained to assume: "The field staff saw itself as playing a very crucial but temporary role in this whole thing. Go into a community. As soon as local leadership begins to emerge, get out of the community, so that the leadership will take hold and people will not continue to turn to you for guidance. You work yourself out of a job rather than trying to maintain yourself in a position or your organization."

Eight

Freedom Rides

During the period that SNCC was concentrating on direct action and voter registration drives, another group, CORE, was planning a direct action campaign called Freedom Rides. James Farmer, a graduate of Howard University, former secretary of FOR, and CORE's national director in 1961, organized the Freedom Rides. He later explained the "intention was to provoke the southern authorities into arresting us and thereby prod the Justice Department into enforcing the law of the land." The law he referred to was the 1960 Supreme Court decision *Boynton v. Virginia*, which further outlawed segregation in all interstate travel facilities, including waiting rooms, bathrooms, and food counters.

The Freedom Rides began on May 4, 1961, in Washington, D.C., and were scheduled to end in New Orleans on May 17, the seventh anniversary of the *Brown v. Board of Education* decision. Seven African Americans and six whites boarded one of two buses—a Trailways or a Greyhound, the two dominant interstate bus companies. One of the participants was John Lewis, son of Alabama sharecroppers, who would become chairman of SNCC in 1963 and a U.S. Congressman in 1986. Another participant was James Peck, a white activist who had participated in the 1947 Journey of Reconciliation, which the Freedom Rides were modeled after.

A 1961 map showing the routes taken during the Freedom Rides. *(Library of Congress)*

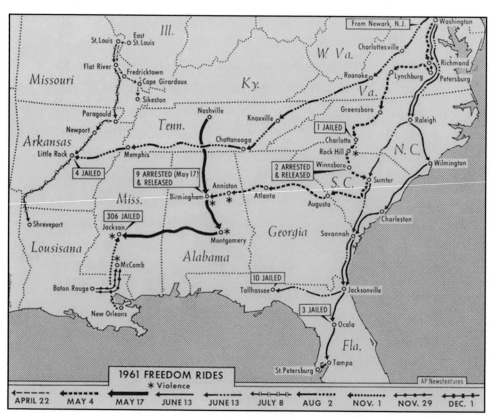

Farmer had sent a letter to President Kennedy informing him of the ride and enclosing a map of the planned route. He asked the president to provide federal protection. He sent similar notifications to the Justice Department, the FBI, and the bus companies.

The Freedom Riders met some resistance in Virginia, and the farther south they traveled, opposition grew more violent. In Rock Hill, South Carolina, Lewis and another rider were beaten and a third rider was arrested for using a whites-only restroom. In Anniston, Alabama, the Greyhound bus was attacked by an angry white mob that smashed windows and slashed tires. Police intervened, and the driver was able to leave, but he had to stop at a gas station some six miles out of town because of flat tires. There the bus was fire bombed, and the riders were forced to escape through emergency exits.

When the Trailways bus stopped in Birmingham, Alabama, angry whites wielding clubs, bricks, iron pipes, and knives attacked the riders without any interference from the police. Some riders were beaten so badly that one eye witness reported he "couldn't see their faces through the blood." Birmingham's Public Safety Commissioner, Eugene "Bull" Connor, explained the absence of police to protect the riders by telling reporters his men were off duty visiting their mothers for Mother's Day. Later, it was learned that Connor had promised the KKK fifteen minutes alone with the riders and that he had instructed them to beat them until "it looked like a bulldog got a hold of them."

The U.S. Department of Justice, under the leadership of President Kennedy's brother and the nation's attorney general, Robert Kennedy, was forced to intervene. Alabama's Governor Patterson refused to promise to protect the buses. He complained, "The citizens of the state are so enraged that I cannot guarantee protection for this bunch of rabble-rousers." James Farmer agreed to the Justice Department's request to evacuate the remaining riders for fear of their lives. It was only a temporary setback.

Diane Nash, who was coleading the SNCC sit-in movement in Nashville, Tennessee, explained, "The students have decided that we can't let violence overcome. We are going to [go] into Birmingham to continue the Freedom Ride." When asked if she realized that riders had almost been killed, she responded, "Yes. That's exactly why the ride must not be stopped. If they stop us with violence, the movement is dead."

Nash and John Lewis led SNCC's resumption of the ride, which was to proceed from Birmingham to Montgomery and then into Mississippi, ending in New Orleans, Louisiana. Organizing the ride, Nash was in constant contact with Ella Baker, who offered suggestions on how the team might better strategize and publicize their efforts, and on how to negotiate with the Justice Department for its intervention and support. She also reminded Nash that the rides themselves were not the point—it was the attention and the momentum that mattered. Baker worked hard behind the scenes to raise money, writing letters to anyone who might be willing to support their cause.

The Freedom Riders continued to meet violent resistance along the way. When the SNCC reinforcements reached the terminal in Montgomery, Alabama, they were again attacked. Some were beaten so severely they sustained permanent injuries. One eyewitness from the Justice Department reported, "The passengers are coming off. A bunch of men led by a guy with a bleeding face are beating them. There are no cops. It's terrible. It's terrible. There's not a cop in sight. People are yelling, 'Get 'em, get 'em.' It's awful."

Attorney General Kennedy pressed Governor Patterson to declare martial law and to escort the riders to the state line under National Guard protection. Patterson finally complied. As the riders crossed into

Attorney General Robert F. Kennedy in 1961. *(Library of Congress)*

Mississippi, National Guardsmen and police took over as escorts. But when the group reached Jackson, Mississippi, the riders were arrested for using the whites-only restrooms. They were taken into custody for their "protection" as part of a compromise negotiated by Attorney General Kennedy. Protection became sixty days in Mississippi's Parchman Penitentiary because the group refused to pay their two hundred dollar fines.

Student activists from all over the country purchased tickets and traveled to Jackson to take the jailed participants' places. Many joined their fellow activists in Mississippi's jails. Their actions resulted in national press coverage. Finally, in November 1961, the Interstate Commerce Commission, under pressure from Attorney General Robert Kennedy, issued new regulations that included penalties for violating the 1960 Supreme Court decision. This was a major victory for SNCC. Not only did the young people take a nonviolent stand and endure hardships and brutality, they brought national attention to the civil rights movement and secured SNCC's standing as a political force. The Freedom Rides were more evidence that direct nonviolent action could produce results.

Meanwhile, SNCC's voter registration efforts were proceeding in McComb, Mississippi, under the direction of Bob Moses. Moses explained that he had "sought the worst part of the most intransigent state" in order "to break the Solid South by applying pressure at its strongest point." Mississippi was widely considered to be the nation's most violently racist state.

Armed with a letter of introduction from Ella Baker, Moses had met with Amzie Moore, vice president of Mississippi's state conference of NAACP branches. Moses's recollection reveals the insight of Baker's philosophy of working with the local leaders to identify what is most important:

> I keep coming back to . . . [Moore's] insight into . . . what it was that would be the key to unlocking the situation in Mississippi. He wasn't distracted by school integration. He was for it but it didn't distract him from the centrality of the right to vote. He wasn't distracted about the integration of public facilities. It was a good thing, but it was not going straight to the heart of what was the trouble in Mississippi. Somehow, in following his guidance there, we stumbled on the key—the right to vote and the political action that ensued.

Registering voters in Mississippi was a daunting challenge. African Americans comprised 45 percent of the population but only 5 percent of the voters. In Pike County, Mississippi, only two hundred of the county's 8,000 African-American adults were registered. In Amite, the figure was 1,000 out of 5,000, and in Walthall, none of the county's 3,000 African Americans were registered to vote.

Progress was counted in single digits. SNCC volunteers and African Americans who helped registration efforts were regularly arrested on trumped-up charges such as disturbing the peace, violating curfew and seg-regation laws, corner lounging (standing in the corner of one's doorway), or gathering in front of a public building. One shotgun-wielding segregationist summed up the majority white opinion in Mississippi: "Niggers 'round here don't need to vote, so you and your damned buddy get out of here. Goddamn it, Nigger! I'll give you one minute to get out of town or I'll kill you!!"

Registering black voters in the Deep South was highly dangerous. Ella Baker was able to draw on her vast circle of contacts to find places for SNCC volunteers to sleep and eat. She also had names of local volunteers who were willing to help prepare detailed maps that showed the locations of the police department or sheriff's office; the roads, creeks, and safe houses; the public buildings and parks; white businesses and black businesses; and friendly and hostile neighborhoods. This helped to keep SNCC's workers safe.

SNCC headquarters established a Wide Area Tele-phone Service (WATS), a telephone service with a flat monthly fee that allowed headquarters to keep track of field secretaries. Daily organizers would send in field reports that included information such as departure time, destination, mode of travel, names in party, ex-pected time of arrival, date and time of next check in, and a summary of events and activities. One WATS report read:

Ella Baker in the early 1960s. *(The Southern Patriot)*

Greenwood, Mississippi: Since February 20, four Negro businesses on the same street as the SNCC office have been destroyed by fire; SNCC field secretary Sam Block was sentenced to 6 months in jail on a charge of 'circulating breach of the peace,' later changed to 'issuing statements calculated to breach the peace'; staff worker James Travis was shot in the head while driving a car near Greenwood; four other

SNCC workers were cut by glass when their car's windshield was shattered by gunshots from a passing car.

Baker received copies of the WATS reports and often traveled to trouble spots to help.

In 1962, Bob Moses created an umbrella organization to coordinate the voter registration efforts of SNCC, CORE, the NAACP, the Urban League, and the SCLC. The group formed was the Council of Federated Organizations (COFO), with Bob Moses as director. SNCC volunteers provided the majority of staff volunteers. They were present in the spring and early summer of 1963 when the South exploded and Jim Crow's hold began to weaken.

Project C, short for Project Confrontation and also known as the Birmingham campaign, was conceptualized by Reverend Fred L. Shuttlesworth. Ella Baker had visited Birmingham in the 1950s and had worked with him to raise money. The project's objective was for the SCLC and Shuttlesworth's group, the Alabama Christian Movement for Human Rights, to hold protest demonstrations in front of white businesses and public facilities in Birmingham, which was chosen for this direct action campaign because of its reputation as one of the most segregated cities in the South.

Shuttlesworth had been lobbying the SCLC to come to Birmingham—nicknamed "Bombingham"—for years. Martin Luther King Jr. and his advisors saw an oppor-

The wreckage of a bomb explosion near the Gaston Motel where Martin Luther King Jr. and leaders of the SCLC were staying during the Birmingham campaign in May, 1963. *(Library of Congress)*

tunity to exploit a divide in the city's white leadership, which was spilt between hard-line and more "moderate" segregationists. Eugene "Bull" Connor, who had allowed the KKK to attack the Freedom Riders in 1961, was still the face of vicious racism in the city.

In early April 1963, some 150 adults staged sit-ins, followed by a march on city hall. Alabama's state supreme court issued an injunction forbidding further demonstrations. The protests failed to gain national attention until Martin Luther King Jr. led a march of about fifty people. By this point, wherever King went, the national media, including network news crews, followed. The marchers were arrested, and King was thrown into solitary confinement. There he wrote his powerful "Letter from a Birmingham Jail" to explain why African Americans could no longer "wait:"

> . . . when you have seen vicious mobs lynch your mothers and fathers at will and drown your sisters and brothers at whim; when you have seen hate-filled policemen curse, kick, brutalize and even kill your black brothers and sisters with impunity; when you see the vast majority of your twenty million Negro brothers smothering in an air-tight cage of poverty in the midst of an affluent society . . . when you are harried by day and haunted by night by the fact that you are a Negro, living constantly at a tip-toe stance, never quite knowing what to expect next, and plagued with inner fears and outer resentments; when you are forever fighting a degenerating sense of 'nobodiness;' then you will understand why it is difficult to wait.

Project C's leadership decided on a new strategy. They needed hundreds of protestors who were not afraid of losing their jobs or suffering some other economic reprisal. After much argument, they decided to use school children. SNCC volunteers moved in to train the children on nonviolent protest techniques. Volunteers would sneer, shove, scream at, punch, and blow smoke in the faces of the youngsters to prepare them for what might happen. Through it all, the students were instructed never to fight back or retaliate in any way, to take the abuse in silence, with grace.

On May 2, some one thousand students filed silently

by white businesses and Birmingham's city government offices. Bull Connor immediately marshaled his forces to disband the peaceful protestors. Nine hundred and fifty-nine were arrested. The next day, more students flooded the streets. Connor ordered police dogs and high-powered fire hoses turned on them. One businessman registered his horror, exclaiming, "They've turned the fire hoses on a little black girl. And they're rolling that girl right down the middle of the street." The attacks on their children caused Birmingham's African-American adults to join the demonstrations in larger numbers than ever before. The nation reacted with outrage. One Maryland woman's response was carried in the *Washington Post* after pictures

Demonstrators practice the discipline of nonviolent resistance as authorities turn high-pressure hoses on them in downtown Birmingham. *(AP Photo / Bill Hudson)*

brought home the horrors of what was happening in Birmingham:

> Now I've seen everything. The news photographer who took that picture of a police dog lunging at a human being has shown us in unmistakable terms how low we have sunk and will surely have awakened a feeling of shame in all who have seen that picture, who have any notion of human dignity. The man being lunged at was not a criminal being tracked down to prevent his murdering other men; he was, and is, a man. If he can have a beast deliberately urged to lunge at him, then so can any man, woman, or child in the United States . . . If the United States doesn't stand for some average decent level of human dignity, what does it stand for?

By May 6, some one thousand young people and 1,500 adults had been jailed. Outdoor pens were erected, with as many as seventy-five students crammed into cells meant to house eight. By May 12, the city was in chaos, and President Kennedy sent 3,000 federal troops to nearby Fort McClellan.

Baker, who was in route to a new job in Louisville, Kentucky, to work as a consultant to the Southern Conference Education Fund (SCEF), headed to Birmingham instead. She was particularly concerned for the students who had been arrested. She visited them in jail and assured them their courage and participation were making a difference. She then joined King and the other leaders to discuss how to resolve the impasse. Eventually, white business leaders agreed to desegregate their businesses, and both sides agreed to establish a committee to address additional desegregation efforts. This victory and the press coverage of the brutal police retaliations brought renewed financial and volunteer support to the civil rights movement.

The children's march marked another level of direct action. Extensive television coverage revealed how segregation actually worked and what it looked like. Despite the attention, segregation continued. Only a few weeks later, the governor of Alabama, George Wallace—whose campaign slogan was "segregation now, segregation tomorrow, segregation forever"—refused to integrate the University of Alabama. It took the National Guard to intercede to have the black students enrolled.

The events in Birmingham began to motivate national leaders to address the problem. In response to Wallace's disregard for the law, President Kennedy demanded fifteen minutes of network time on television to address the nation to say:

> We preach freedom around the world and we mean it. And we cherish our freedom here at home. But are we to say to the world—and much more importantly, to each other—that this is the land of the free except for Negroes; that we have no second-class citizens, except Negroes; that we have no class or cast system, no ghettos, no master race, except with respect to Negroes.

Now the time has come for the nation to fulfill its

> promise. The events in Birmingham and elsewhere have so increased the cries for equality that no city or state or legislative body can prudently ignore them. . . . We face, therefore, a moral crisis, as a country and a people. It cannot be met by repressive police action. It cannot be left to increased demonstrations in the streets. It cannot be quieted by token moves or talks. It is time to act in the Congress, in your state and local legislative bodies, in all of our daily lives.

Kennedy then announced that he was submitting a civil rights bill to Congress, saying, "We owe them, and we owe ourselves, a better country." The president's stand finally brought the federal government squarely into the civil rights debate. A few days later, the president pulled a note from his pocket, telling those in his presence that it was the results of the latest poll, which showed his national support had plummeted thirteen percentage points, from 60 to 47 percent. His only comment was, "I may lose the next election because of this. I don't care."

The victory in Birmingham and the intervention of President Kennedy did not end the violence. The day after the president's address, June 12, 1963, Medgar Evers, Baker's old friend from the Mississippi NAACP, was murdered on his own front lawn. It took thirty-one years to bring his killer, Byron De La Beckwith, a leader in the White Citizens' Council, to justice.

That fall, at 10:19 AM on September 15, 1963, a bomb

Onlookers view the bomb-damaged home of Arthur Shores, NAACP attorney, in Birmingham, Alabama, on September 5, 1963. *(Library of Congress)*

exploded in the basement of the 16th Street Baptist Church in Birmingham, Alabama. The church was a gathering place for many mass meetings and the head-quarters for demonstrations. The blast killed four young school girls—eleven-year-old Denise McNair and four-teen-year-olds Addie Mae Collins, Carole Robertson, and Cynthia Wesley—and injured twenty others.

The Birmingham office of the FBI investigated and identified four white men, all Ku Klux Klan members, as suspects, and recommended they be prosecuted. But FBI Director J. Edgar Hoover blocked their prosecution. He even claimed civil rights activists had planted the bomb in order to garner public sympathy and support.

The Congress of Racial Equality (CORE) conducts a march in memory of the four African-American girls killed in the Birmingham church bombing—Washington, D.C., September 22, 1963. *(Library of Congress)*

One suspect was tried in 1977 and convicted of murder, but it took forty years before two separate juries found the two remaining men guilty of murder and sentenced them to life in prison. The fourth suspect died before he could be brought to trial.

Nine

Getting Out the Vote

During the summer of 1963, SNCC volunteers poured into Mississippi to help with the Freedom Vote campaign. Because many Americans were not aware African Americans were denied the vote in Mississippi, COFO decided to hold a mock voter registration and election. The goal was to demonstrate that, if given a chance, African Americans would register and vote. Baker went to Mississippi to lend a hand.

Under Baker's guidance, SNCC's young canvassers set to work. Baker's hard work in teaching her young colleagues patience paid off. An observer noted how the SNCC workers performed: "I have seen people slam doors in his face, but he said I'm going to be back. . . . He'd go every day, every hour, every week. Like he would knock on that person's door, they would see him at least 3 or

4 times a week. He'd say, 'This is something you should do. It's free and won't cost you nothing. I got the gas, I got a ride—you ain't got to walk. I've got the paper here. . . . I'll hold your hand.'"

On election day, some 90,000 Mississippians, including 10,000 whites, cast their ballots at voting booths set up in beauty parlors, funeral homes, barbershops, and

The polls in Miami, Florida, on Election Day, 1963, where African Americans could vote. *(Library of Congress)*

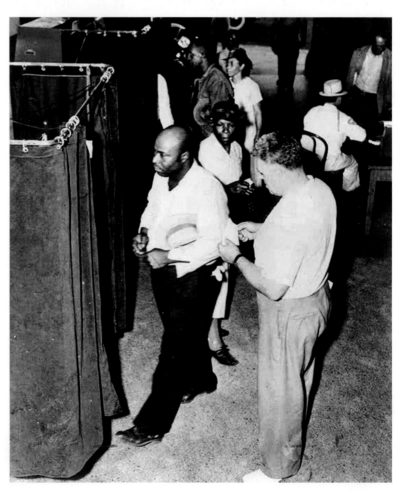

other businesses run by African Americans for the Freedom Vote Mock Election. Their ballots listed the names
of the actual candidates as well as candidates from the
interracial Freedom Party, a party formed for the mock
election. The Freedom Party candidates won handily.
Three times the number of actual registered African-
American voters turned out. Baker declared that the
results clearly refuted the whites' claim that African
Americans were not voting because they were not interested.

As the movement built momentum, A. Philip Randolph
and Bayard Rustin unveiled their idea for the March on
Washington for Jobs and Freedom. The threat of a march
had been used to pressure presidents into offering civil
rights concessions before. This time, Rustin and Randolph
planned to bring people to the National Mall to demand
the passage of the pending Civil Rights Bill, an end to
segregation in public schools, protection for demonstrators against police brutality, a two-dollar-per-hour
minimum wage, the withholding of federal funds from
programs in which racial discrimination existed, and an
enforcement of the Fourteenth Amendment.

Roy Wilkins of the NAACP, James Farmer of CORE,
John Lewis of SNCC, Whitney Young Jr. of the Urban
League, and Martin Luther King Jr. of the SCLC joined
Randolph and Rustin to organize the march, planned for
August 28, 1963.

Rustin, Ella Baker's longtime friend, was named chief
coordinator of the march. One hundred thousand people

were expected, but on August 28, a crowd estimated at 250,000 (a quarter of whom were white) gathered before the Lincoln Memorial. It was the largest political demonstration ever to take place in the United States. Participants came from all over the nation. Celebrities and singers shared the podium with legislators and leaders of the various organizations. A. Philip Randolph opened the demonstration, saying, "Fellow Americans, we are gathered here in the largest demonstration in the history of this nation. Let the nation and the world know the meaning of our numbers. We are not a pressure group, we are not an organization or a group of organizations, we are not a mob. We are the advance guard of a massive moral revolution for jobs and freedom."

John Lewis, now chairman of SNCC, addressed the demonstrators: "By the force of our demands, our determination and our numbers, we shall splinter the segregated South into a thousand pieces, and put them back together in the image of God and Democracy."

The most remembered speech of that day was Martin Luther King Jr.'s "I Have a Dream": "I have a dream that my four children will one day live in a nation where they will not be judged by the color of their skin, but by the content of their character. . . . I have a dream that one day down in Alabama . . . little black boys and black girls will be able to join hands with little white boys and white girls as brothers and sisters."

Opposite: Crowds packed the mall on August 28, 1963, for the March on Washington for Jobs and Freedom. *(National Archives)*

The march was one of the first events to be broadcast internationally via Telstar, the country's first communications satellite. All three major U.S. television networks covered it, and CBS canceled its regular daytime programming to broadcast the event "gavel to gavel." In a poignant turn of events, it was announced at the gathering that on that very day, W. E. B. Du Bois had died in Ghana, fifty-four years after he had cofounded the NAACP to fight segregation and discrimination.

Despite the importance of the day, Baker was not at the march. None of the primary female leaders—Diane Nash, JoAnn Robinson, Ella Baker, Rosa Parks, Pauli Murray, or Septima Poinsette Clark—had been included in the planning group or scheduled to speak. When the march leaders met with President Kennedy at the White House that day, no female leaders were present.

The success of the Freedom Vote in November 1963, prompted SNCC to join forces with COFO to again focus on Mississippi. Over the summer of 1964, what they dubbed Freedom Summer was to consist of an aggressive campaign to register voters, open Freedom Schools, and to organize the Mississippi Freedom Democratic Party.

Ella Baker, at the age of sixty, was to continue in her role as logistical coordinator and consultant to SNCC's leaders and volunteers. Baker said, "One of the reasons we're going into Mississippi is that the rest of the United States has never felt much responsibility for what happens in the Deep South. The country feels no responsi-

An all-male group of march organizers meet with President Kennedy at the White House. A. Philip Randolph is at the center, next to Kennedy. Martin Luther King Jr. is third from the left. *(National Archives)*

bility and doesn't see that as an indictment. Young people will make the Justice Department move. . . . If we can simply let the concept that the rest of the nation bears responsibility for what happens in Mississippi sink in, then we will have accomplished something."

One of the group's new strategies was to actively recruit white students. SNCC "came to the conclusion that it was a necessary political move to invite white students to participate in the program. They were very aware that when a black person got brutalized for attempting to register to vote, this was nothing new, it had been done before. But when the . . . daughter and son of people up North . . . who had some political clout got involved, it was a challenge to the powers that be," said Baker.

More than seven hundred mostly white students attended a weeklong training session in Oxford, Ohio. One program speaker, a Mississippi lawyer who represented civil rights workers as clients, cautioned the students on the importance of following a nonviolent, nonconfrontational approach: "Mississippi is not the place to start conducting constitutional law classes for the policemen, many of whom don't have a fifth-grade education." CORE's James Forman spoke bluntly about the dangers they faced: "I may be killed. You may be killed."

Two hundred new recruits headed to Mississippi in June to pair up with seasoned African-American SNCC and COFO volunteers in biracial teams. The day after the first group arrived, three of the students failed to report to the Freedom Summer headquarters. Instead of looking for the students—James Chaney, Andrew Goodman, and Michael Schwerner—the local sheriff accused them of staging a publicity stunt by disappearing. Under direction from Attorney General Robert F. Kennedy, hundreds of soldiers and FBI agents were assigned to search for them. Six weeks later, the students' bodies were found in an earthen dam on a farm near Philadelphia, Mississippi.

The long search, and the FBI's involvement, brought

six weeks of extensive media coverage. When Baker was asked by one reporter for a comment, she said, "The unfortunate thing is that it took this . . . to make the rest of the country turn its eyes on the fact that there were other [black] bodies lying under the swamps of Mississippi. Until the killing of a black mother's son becomes as important as the killing of white mother's son, we who believe in freedom cannot rest."

The FBI arrested twenty-one white men, including the county sheriff and deputy sheriff, for the murders. All were acquitted by an all-white jury. Edgar Ray Killen, a Baptist minister and former Klan leader, was indicted for the murders in January 2005 and stood trial later that spring.

In the middle of all this, President Johnson, who had become president when John F. Kennedy was assassinated on November 22, 1963, signed the Civil Rights Act in July 1964. The historic bill outlawed segregation in public areas and required the federal government to help communities integrate schools. It also created the Equal Employment Opportunity Commission (EEOC) to oversee the portion of the legislation that prohibited discrimination in hiring, wages, and promotion based on sex, color, creed, or national origin. But the act did nothing to ensure the voting rights of African Americans.

This prompted civil rights leaders to urge legislators to pass both the Twenty-fourth Amendment and a new Voting Rights Act. The Twenty-fourth Amendment

VOTING IN ALABAMA

A sample 1950s voting application form from Alabama was four pages long and, among other things, asked applicants, almost always only blacks, to list their last five years' of addresses, the place of birth of their spouse, their last five years of work history, and to swear that they were not a member of a group planning to overthrow the U.S. government. The form also asked for the names and addresses of two witnesses who could vouch for the applicant.

After completing this form, the applicant was required to take a literacy test. There were over one hundred tests in circulation, making it difficult for civil rights workers to adequately prepare aspiring voters. Some sample questions from a test: If a person charged with treason denies his guilt, how many persons must testify against him before he can be convicted? (Answer: two) Name one area of authority over state militia reserved exclusively to the states. (Answer: the appointment of officers) In what year did Congress gain the right to prohibit the migration of persons to the states? (Answer: 1808) If the United States wishes to purchase land for an arsenal and have exclusive legislative authority over it, consent is required from the _____ (Answer: legislature).

Finally, after filling out forms and taking tests (including reading a section of the Constitution out loud and possibly answering questions about it), applicants were sent home and told they would be notified if the Board of Registrars accepted or denied their application. The board reviewed applications in secret and could deny an applicant without explanation. The name of every person who applied to vote was published in the newspaper for two weeks running.

guaranteed that the voting rights of every American citizen "shall not be denied or abridged by the United States or any state by reason of failure to pay any poll tax or other tax."

President Lyndon Johnson signs the Civil Rights Bill into law on July 2, 1964.

Meanwhile, in Mississippi, the struggle between the Freedom Summer volunteers and the segregationist power structure continued. The Mississippi state legislature tired to stamp out the organizers by passing a "bill to restrain movements of individuals under certain circumstances;" Jackson's mayor purchased an armed tank; and the KKK burned crosses in three-quarters of the state's counties.

At the same time, the Freedom Summer volunteers established over fifty freedom schools to supplement the education of African Americans. Freedom schools focused on improving literacy skills and instilling basic political and citizenship skills. Many of the techniques used were patterned after those developed by Septima Clark, another of Baker's friends since the Highlander Folk School days. Clark had cofounded the Citizenship School program in the late 1950s, which had eventually been moved under the SCLC's umbrella. It was a grassroots program that trained local leaders to be Citizenship School teachers, who in turn taught their fellow community members to read and write enough to pass some of the southern states' literacy tests.

The third objective for Freedom Summer was to form the Mississippi Freedom Democratic Party (MFDP). At its state convention, the all-white Mississippi Democratic Party had declared: "[We] believe in the segregation of the races, and are unalterably opposed to the repeal or modification of the segregation laws of this State, and . . . condemn integration and the practice of non-segregation." Though the Supreme Court's 1944 ruling in *Smith v. Allwright* forced political parties to allow black voters to vote in primary elections, many state parties remained segregated. The MFDP planned to go to the upcoming national convention in Atlantic City and to insist on being seated as the real representatives of the Mississippi Democratic Party. Before leaving for Atlantic City, the MFDP held a state convention in Jackson, Mississippi.

Ella Baker was the keynote speaker. During her speech she said that the goal of their party was too "demand to be let into America." She was appointed executive director and had earlier set up the MFDP office in Washington, D.C. Her extensive network of contacts was indispensable to the MFDP as she sought help from all corners. She lobbied everyone she knew in the national Democratic Party and pressured them to vote to seat the MFDP instead of the segregated "official" delegates at the convention.

Roughly 60,000 Mississippians registered with the MFDP. The vice chairperson of the MFDP delegation to the national convention was Fannie Lou Hamer. The youngest of twenty children born to sharecroppers in Montgomery County, Mississippi, Hamer had married a farmhand with whom she lived and worked a parcel of land of a former cotton plantation near Ruleville, Mississippi. She had attended a mass meeting put on by SNCC in the summer of 1962 and then tried to register to vote in Indianola, the county seat. She and sixteen others were denied registration. When she returned home, she and her husband were thrown out of their house and off of the land they had worked for eighteen years. Hamer later said about this attempt to punish her, "They set me free. It's the best thing that could happen. Now I can work for my people."

Hamer turned her efforts toward the voter registration drive in Mississippi. She was working in the field for SNCC under Bob Moses when she was arrested for trying to register black voters. Her white jailers ordered two African-American prisoners to beat her or face a beating themselves:

Three white men came into my room. One was a state highway policeman (he had the marking on his sleeve). ... They said they were going to make me wish I was dead. They made me lay down on my face and they ordered two Negro prisoners to beat me with a blackjack. That was unbearable. The first prisoner beat me until he was exhausted, then the second Negro began to beat me. I had polio when I was about six years old. I was limp. I was holding my hands behind me to protect my weak side. ..... They beat me until my body was hard, 'til I couldn't bend my fingers or get up when they told me to. That's how I got this blood clot in my eye—the sight's nearly gone now. My kidney was injured from the blows they gave me on the back.

Two years later, when Hamer went before the Democratic Party Credentials Committee in Atlantic City to explain why the MFDP should be invited to sit at the convention, she told them of this experience. At the end of her comments she asked the delegates, "Is this America? Is this the land of the free; is this the home of the brave?" Hamer's speech became the lead story on that evening's television news broadcasts.

Suddenly the conflict over seating the MFDP was the big story out of the 1964 Democratic Convention. Earlier in the summer, the Republicans had nominated Senator Barry Goldwater of Arizona to run for president. Goldwater had voted against the 1964 Civil Rights Act and was hoping to gain white support by promising to roll back the progress on civil rights. Few had thought Goldwater had a chance of winning in November, but now that the Democratic Party faced the prospect of a failed convention because of the conflict over the Mississippi delegation, Goldwater's victory seemed more possible. The delegations from other southern states, such as Alabama, Georgia, and President Johnson's home state of Texas, threatened to join Mississippi in a walkout if the MFDP was seated. Using the language of the day, *Newsweek* magazine summarized the party's and President Johnson's dilemma: "To disregard the Negro's demands would be to repudiate the moral drive of the Negro revolution; to satisfy them would mean a floor fight almost certain to trigger a southern walkout."

Focused on winning the election, President Johnson was bitter about having his crowning convention disrupted. He had signed the 1964 Civil Rights Act on July 2, less than two months before the convention was to begin. The act outlawed legal segregation throughout the nation, and Johnson pushed it through Congress at great political cost. Johnson argued that he had done more to advance civil rights than any president since Abraham Lincoln. He knew that the Democratic Party would lose millions of votes from white Southerners over the next generation because of his support of civil rights and he felt that he should have earned the loyalty of African Americans. Instead, he faced a bitter fight that could splinter his party.

Johnson had the leaders of the convention offer a compromise. The MFDP delegates would be seated as guests without voting privileges, and the convention would pass a resolution barring any future convention from seating white-only delegations. Ella Baker and other MFDP leaders rejected the president's offer.

Two days later, the president's representatives were back with another compromise. The MFDP could have two at-large seats, as official members, but still no voting privileges. The white-only Mississippi delegation would be integrated, but the black members would not have any power. This second offer was argued over by the MFDP party and other African-American leaders. Martin Luther King Jr., Bayard Rustin, and Roy Wilkins wanted to accept it. They had worked with President Johnson in the past and knew they would have to work with him in the future. To them, the MFDP fight was only one of many battles in a long war. This compromise would allow them to have a unified convention and hopefully assure Johnson's election. Then they could begin pushing for a voting rights act, the next critical part of national legislation.

Ella Baker and Fannie Lou Hamer rejected the offer as a meaningless token. They had not come to Atlantic City to accept a face-saving compromise, they argued. Baker spoke out against it in a straightforward style that castigated the behind-the-scenes maneuvering that arrived at the compromise. She argued that the delegates had been sent to represent the people of Mississippi and

Mississippi Freedom Democratic Party delegates sing on the boardwalk in Atlantic City outside the Democratic National Convention in 1964. Fannie Lou Hamer holds the microphone. Ella Baker stands to the far right. Stokely Carmichael is pictured in the rear in a straw hat. *(© 1976 George Ballis / Take Stock)*

could not have their rights negotiated away by a few leaders. She insisted the entire MFDP delegation should be seated with full voting rights.

After bitter arguments, the compromise was rejected. The MFDP party was barred from the convention. They joined other protestors from SNCC and CORE outside and attempted to block the entrances so delegates could not enter. Most of the white Mississippi delegation had long since walked out, angered at the prospect of even having to sit with African Americans. A few people, including Fannie Lou Hamer, later sneaked onto the floor and sat in chairs reserved for their state delegation. But these protests were still only symbolic acts. The MFDP had been barred from participating in the national convention of the political party to which they had given their allegiance.

Baker did not see the rejection of the MFDP as a defeat. The experience confirmed her belief that to change the system, it would be necessary to work from the outside. The 1964 Democratic Convention marked the beginning of a shift in the civil rights movement. The more mainstream part of the movement, such as that represented by the SCLC and the NAACP, would continue to work for legal and legislative change within the two-party system and the national and state governments, and would maintain a commitment to nonviolence. At the same time, a radical movement advocating more rapid change would begin to operate outside the halls of government.

Initially, much of this division within the civil rights movement would happen within SNCC. Eventually, the conflict between the moderate and radical elements would put the group Ella Baker had helped to found and nurture under intense strain.

Ten

Fundi

After the 1964 Democratic Convention, members of SNCC met in Atlanta to decide what to do next. The group was spilt over how and where to focus its energies. Baker did her best to mediate between the various factions. A second meeting, at which Baker was not present, saw tensions develop between SNCC's white and black members, as some African Americans began to suggest there was no place for white people in their movement. These comments were not well received by white volunteers who had worked for civil rights for years, and tensions again arose.

President Johnson easily defeated Goldwater in November 1964 and immediately began to pressure Congress to continue to enact laws designed to better the lives of American citizens—including a Voting Rights

Act that would guarantee African Americans the right to vote and antipoverty legislation to increase funding for housing, education, and food programs.

Despite the conflict within SNCC and between it and the SCLC, the groups agreed to work together to support the Voting Rights Act which was then winding its way through Congress and would eventually grant voting rights to all African Americans. The strategy they planned, which was intended to bring the nation's attention to the barriers placed on voting in the South, was a march from Selma, Alabama, to the state capital in Montgomery. Selma was chosen as the place to begin the march demanding voting rights for a simple, startling reason. Only 1.9 percent of African Americans eligible to vote in Selma and surrounding Dallas County were registered. African Americans were the majority population in the county, and white leaders had worked hard to keep them off the voter rolls. This made it exactly the type of place Baker, King, and other civil rights leaders wanted to expose to the rest of the country—and the world.

On the eve of the scheduled march, however, Martin Luther King Jr. called it off. Alabama governor George Wallace, who had run for election as a segregationist, insisted that the march would not be tolerated. It was a clear threat of force. King, who had been meeting frequently with President Johnson to draft a voting rights act, argued that it was best to delay the march. After the decision was made, King left for Atlanta. SNCC's John

Demonstrators, some carrying American flags, participate in the civil rights march from Selma to Montgomery, Alabama, in 1965. *(Library of Congress)*

Lewis disagreed with the decision and urged the SCLC coordinator who worked in Selma, Hosea Williams, to proceed anyway. He promised SNCC's support if the march continued.

Williams agreed. On Sunday, March 7, 1965, six hundred people began their march through the streets of Selma. After six blocks, the marchers turned to cross the Alabama River on the steel Edmund Pettus Bridge. The bridge was so narrow it forced the marchers into walking two to three abreast. As the front of the group, led by Williams and Lewis, topped the bridge's crest, they saw stretching before them on the opposite side of the river a barricade made up of state troopers dressed in riot gear, complete with helmets. Backing up the troops were dozens of white vigilantes that had been deputized by the local sheriff. The vigilantes carried whips, sticks, clubs, and other weapons. Several carried the Confederate battle flag that had become a symbol of white resistance to civil rights.

The marchers stopped at the bridge's end and asked to speak with the commander of the state troops. He refused to talk with them and announced they had two minutes to disperse. Lewis and the others at the front of the march then knelt to pray. They expected to be arrested. Instead, the police, followed by the laughing and cheering vigilantes, waded into the unarmed marchers wielding clubs, whips, cattle prods, chains, and tear gas. Fortunately, television cameras captured the attack. The ensuing news coverage generated massive public attention, sympathy, and outrage. That day soon became known as Bloody Sunday.

The outcry against the state-sponsored brutality created a wave of sympathy for the marchers. Six days later, President Lyndon Johnson invited Governor George Wallace to the White House. As one witness recalled, the tall president put his arm around the diminutive Wallace's shoulder and said, "It's a moment in history, and how do we want to be remembered in history? Do we want to be remembered as petty little men, or do we want to be remembered as great figures that faced up to our moments of crises?"

The following Monday, the president addressed the nation and a joint session of Congress to advocate for passage of the voting rights bill. "It's wrong—deadly wrong—to deny any of your fellow Americans the right to vote," he said. President Johnson went on to say, "Even if we pass this bill, the battle will not be over. What happened in Selma is part of a far larger movement which reaches into every section and every state of America. It is an effort of American Negroes to secure for themselves the full blessings of American life. Their cause must be our cause too. It is not just Negroes, but all of us, who must overcome the crippling legacy of bigotry and injustice. And, we *shall* overcome!"

Two days later, Federal District Court Judge Frank M.

In addition to refusing to protect the Selma marchers, Governor George Wallace gained significant notoriety as an anti-integrationist when he defiantly blocked the doorway of the University of Alabama from African-American students seeking entrance in June 1963. *(Library of Congress)*

Johnson Jr. issued a ruling in response to SNCC and SCLC's petition to secure federal protection for another attempt to march from Selma to Montgomery. It read: "The law is clear that the right to petition one's government for the redress of grievances may be exercised in large groups . . . and these rights may be exercised by marching, even along public highways."

Governor Wallace still refused to provide protection for the marchers, so President Johnson federalized 2,000 Alabama National Guard troops. These men, along with another 2,000 Army troops, one hundred FBI agents, and one hundred federal marshals, were ordered to protect the marchers.

Sunday, March 21, approximately 3,200 marchers left Selma and walked about twelve miles a day, sleeping in fields along the way, until they reached Montgomery, fifty-four miles later. As they approached the capitol steps, the group had swelled to some 25,000 white and black people.

Five months later, President Johnson signed the Voting Rights Act into law. It prohibited the denial or abridgment of a person's right to vote on account of race or color. Finally, Jim Crow laws, practices, and procedures with regards to voting rights were rendered illegal by the federal government. One million African Americans registered to vote after passage of the 1965 Voting Rights Act, and by 1972, two African Americans from the South had been elected to the United States Congress.

Ella Baker speaking on behalf of the Southern Conference Educational Fund at a news conference in the late 1960s. *(AP Photo)*

Ella Baker had supported SNCC's participation at Selma. She was pleased that the Voting Rights Act, which her years of work had helped make possible, was finally the law of the land.

By 1965, however, Baker was sixty-one years old and was beginning to tire from the decades of constant travel and struggle. She could no longer maintain the pace she had for so many years. She was also growing wary of the conflict within SNCC. She decided to return to her apartment in Harlem.

In June of 1966, the tension within SNCC erupted into open conflict. John Lewis was defeated in a vote for another term as leader by the more radical Stokely Carmichael, who had popularized the phrase "Black Power" at rallies. Baker had empathy for Carmichael, because she knew what it felt like to struggle to make her voice heard. While many of the other older leaders, including Bayard Rustin, rejected the increasing militancy of Carmichael and his supporters, Baker understood their anger. She did not agree with Carmichael's calls for black separatism, however, and maintained a carefully noncommittal stance toward the movement to reject whites from membership in SNCC.

Stokely Carmichael, photographed here at age twenty-five, became the head of SNCC in 1966. He introduced the phrase "Black Power" to the civil rights movement, alienating many older activists and organizers. *(AP Photo)*

In the winter of 1966, a movement was initiated to eject the last of the few remaining white workers in SNCC. Many had already left when they were made to feel unwelcome, but a few had hung on, including Bob Zellner and his wife, Dorothy. Committed SNCC activists since its inception, the Zellners had been arrested multiple times. Yet they were to be kicked out by members who felt there was no place for them there. On the way to what would be his final SNCC meeting, Baker was the one to break the news to Bob Zellner. Though she did not support the ejection of white members, she wanted to prepare Zellner for what he was about to hear. As a result of that December meeting, the Zellners left SNCC to join the staff of the Southern Conference Education Fund (SCEF), another of the organizations Baker supported.

In the coming years, Baker continued to lend a hand to the movement wherever she could, as she withdrew even more from public life. Her occasional returns were often dramatic, including a 1969 speech called "The Black Woman in the Civil Rights Struggle." She spoke feelingly about her experiences with discrimination within the movement and urged her audience to consider the plight of women. She devoted increasing amounts of time to women's issues and shared the podium with Betty Friedan, one of the founders of the National Organization for Women (NOW), at the 1975 International Women's Day celebrations in New York.

Among other causes Baker worked to support was

Feminist and activist Betty Friedan. *(Library of Congress)*

Puerto Rican independence. She was also pleased to see the civil rights movement expand to incorporate causes of independence around the globe, including in South Africa.

Baker was the keynote speaker at a 1974 rally for Puerto Rican independence at Madison Square Garden. In her speech, she recalled her reaction to the young white boy who had called her a "nigger" when she was six years old. She said, "I hit him. But then I learned that hitting back at one person was not enough." She continued, "You and I cannot be free in America or anywhere else where there is capitalism and imperialism, until we can get people to recognize that they themselves have to make the struggle and the fight for freedom every day in the year, every year until they win it."

In the last decade of her life, Ella Baker received a number of awards and honors. She was also honored with a seventy-fifth birthday celebration at the Carnegie Endowment for Peace in New York City, where hundreds gathered to pay their respects, including celebrities, politicians, civil rights leaders, and volunteers. Between 1979 and 1981, Baker worked with Joanne Grant on a documentary film of her life called *Fundi*. Grant took the title from a Swahili word for a person who passes their knowledge of a craft to the next generation.

Over time Ella Baker's weary body began to fail. She was diagnosed with Alzheimer's disease in the late 1970s and became increasingly confined to her apartment. Then, on December, 13, 1986, her eighty-third birthday, Ella Josephine Baker died in her Harlem apartment.

Over her lifetime, Ella Baker had participated in or cofounded scores of organizations, campaigns, and alliances in the fight for civil rights for African Americans and other oppressed peoples. "I was never working for an organization; I have always tried to work for a cause. And the cause to me is bigger than any organization, bigger than any group of people. It is the cause of humanity. . . . The drive of the *human* spirit for freedom," she once said.

Though she had rejected a career as a teacher, Baker's ultimate legacy is the wisdom and experience she offered to all she encountered. Ella Baker once said, "If there is any philosophy, it's that those who have walked a certain path should know some things, should remember some things that they can pass on, that others can use to walk the path a little better." Her life was a testament to this philosophy and to the power one individual has to effect change. As for the future, Baker once said, "I believe that the struggle is eternal. Someone else carries on," and, over time, these individual efforts can become a force of "crusading proportions," a force for revolutionary change.

Timeline

1903   Ella Baker is born December 13, Norfolk, Virginia.

1918   Enrolls in Shaw Academy and University.

1927   Graduates from Shaw University in April; moves to New York City.

1930   Cofounds the Young Negroes' Cooperative Council; serves as YNCL's national executive director.

1939   Marries T. J. (Bob) Roberts.

1940   Assistant field secretary for the NAACP.

1943   Made NAACP's director of branches.

1947   Helps organize the Journey for Reconciliation.

1952   Elected president of the New York City branch of the NAACP.

1955   Cofounds In Friendship and serves as its executive secretary.

1957   Helps organize the Southern Christian Leadership Conference (SCLC).

1958   Appointed as SCLC's interim executive director.

1960   Helps found SNCC; resigns as interim executive director of SCLC to serve as advisor to SNCC.

1964   Cofounds the Mississippi Freedom Democratic Party (MFDP) and appointed its executive director.

1971 Returns to Harlem.
1979 Begins work on a documentary film of her life, *Fundi*.
1985 Receives honorary doctorate from City College of New York.
1986 Dies on her eighty-third birthday, December 13.

Sources

CHAPTER ONE: Deep Roots

p. 9, "the mistress wanted . . ." Barbara Ransby, *Ella Baker and the Black Freedom Movement* (Chapel Hill: The University of North Carolina Press, 2003), 22.

p. 11, "started throwing [them] . . . fight back," Joanne Grant, *Ella Baker, Freedom Bound* (New York: John Wiley & Sons, Inc., 1998), 16.

p. 13, "to enforce social . . ." Sanford Wexler, *The Civil Rights Movement: An Eyewitness History* (New York: Facts on File, 1993), 6.

p. 18, "two-ness . . . born with a veil," W. E. B. Du Bois, *The Souls of Black Folk,* Bartleby.com, http://www.bartleby.com/114/1.html (accessed March 31, 2005).

p. 19, "It is a peculiar sensation . . ." Ibid.

p. 19-20, "to achieve, through . . ." Wexler, *The Civil Rights Movement,* 9.

p. 20, "The wisest among . . ." Stanley K. Schultz, "Lecture 09: The Great Migration: Blacks in White America," American History 102: Civil War to the Present, University of Wisconsin, http://us.history.wisc.edu/hist102/lectures/lecture09.html (accessed March 31, 2005).

p. 21, "that in the great leap . . ." Norman Coombs, "Chapter 8, The Crisis of Leadership," *The Black Experience in America: The Immigrant Heritage of America* (1993), www.usc.edu/isd/archives/ethnicstudies/historicdocs/ Coombs/coombs_chap8.txt (accessed March 31, 2005).

p. 21-22, "The Negro race, like . . ." Ibid.

p. 23, "He was the one . . ." Grant, *Ella Baker,* 13.

p. 23, "was a work house . . ." Shyrlee Dallard, *Ella Baker: A Leader Behind the Scenes* (Englewood Cliffs, NJ: Silver Burdett Press, Inc., 1990), 23.

p. 24, "[In] my grandpa's . . ." Grant, *Ella Baker,* 7.

CHAPTER TWO: Littleton

p. 25, "There was a deep . . ." Dallard, *Ella Baker: A Leader Behind the Scenes,* 17 & 19.

p. 25, "there was no . . ." Charles M. Payne, *I've Got the Light of Freedom: The Organizing Tradition and the Mississippi Freedom Struggle* (Berkeley: University of California Press, 1995), 80-81.

p. 25, "We were the kind . . ." Ransby, *Ella Baker and the Black Freedom Movement,* 20.

p. 26, "[m]any a night . . ." Dallard, *Ella Baker: A Leader Behind the Scenes,* 19.

p. 27, "The manner in which . . ." Ransby, *Ella Baker and the Black Freedom Movement,* 39-40.

p. 28, "[W]e went to school . . ." Ibid., 32-33.

p. 29, "largely with an old . . ." Ransby, *Ella Baker and the Black Freedom Movement,* 47.

p. 29, "unblemished moral character . . . at [the] institution," Ibid., 52.

p. 29, "no frivolous conversations . . ." Ibid.

p. 29, "helped to win . . . " Ibid., 55.

p. 31, "felt it was their . . ." Ibid., 60.

p. 32, "I didn't seem . . ." Ibid.

p. 32, "contradictions in what . . ." Grant, *Ella Baker,* 23.

p. 32, "My man-woman . . ." Ransby, *Ella Baker and the Black Freedom Movement,* 56-57.

p. 32-33, "You know how men . . ." Ibid., 57.

p. 33, "Awake youth of the . . ." Ibid., 63.

p. 34, "couldn't teach unless . . ." Ibid., 62.

p. 34, "a demeaning sort of thing . . ." Ibid.

CHAPTER THREE: Harlem

p. 37, "Try to imagine . . ." Wexler, *The Civil Rights Movement,* 25.

p. 37, "exotic, colorful, and . . ." Grant, *Ella Baker,* 27.

p. 40, "I went everywhere . . ." Payne, *I've Got the Light of Freedom,* 82.

p. 44, "If you hadn't stood . . ." Ransby, *Ella Baker and the Black Freedom Movement,* 69.

p. 46, "economic salvation," Ibid., 82.

p. 46, "gain economic power . . ." Ibid., 83.

p. 46, "for the common good . . . combat slums," Ibid., 86.

p. 46, "second emancipation," Ibid., 87.

p. 46-47, "awaken the Negro . . ." Grant, *Ella Baker,* 34.

p. 47, "Miss Baker will . . ." Ibid.

p. 48, "social, economic . . ." Ransby, *Ella Baker and the Black Freedom Movement,* 70.

p. 49, "The main objective . . ." Grant, *Ella Baker: Freedom Bound,* 38.

p. 51, "organization of organizations . . ." *Encyclopedia Britannica Online,* "National Council of Negro Women," Women in American, http://www.britannica.com/women/articles/National_Council_of_Negro_Women.html (accessed March 31, 2005).

p. 52, "out of his . . .she had hers," Ransby, *Ella Baker and the Black Freedom Movement,* 103.

p. 52, "I had it all . . ." Ibid., 102.

p. 53, "It was one . . ." Ibid.

p. 53, "Many people didn't . . ." Ibid.

p. 53, "relate to people and share . . ." Grant, *Ella Baker,* 224.

CHAPTER FOUR: The NAACP

p. 57, "to place the NAACP . . ." Ransby, *Ella Baker and the Black Freedom Movement,* 112.

p. 57, "thirty-eight branches . . ." Grant, *Ella Baker,* 49.

p. 57, "We must have the..." Ibid.

p. 57-58, "visiting barber . . . and grilles," Ransby, *Ella Baker and the Black Freedom Movement,* 112.

p. 58, "a powerful speaker . . ." Ibid. 131.

p. 58, "depended on both . . ." Dallard, *Ella Baker: A Leader Behind the Scenes,* 46.

p. 59, "One of the most . . . " Ransby, *Ella Baker and the Black Freedom Movement,* 115.

p. 60, "hoping and waiting . . ." Grant, *Ella Baker,* 49.

p. 60-61, "What are the . . ." Ibid., 54.

p. 61, "take that one thing . . ." Ibid.

p. 63, "The French had a . . ." Richard Wormser, "The Rise and Fall of Jim Crow—Jim Crow Stories—U.S. in World War II (1941-45)," PBS.org, http://www.pbs.org/wnet/jimcrow/ stories_events_ww2.html (accessed March 31, 2005).

p. 63, "We thought it . . ." Ibid.

p. 64, "The right to vote in a . . ." Richard Wormser, "The Rise and Fall of Jim Crow—Jim Crow Stories—Smith v. Allright (1944)," PBS.org, http://www.pbs.org/wnet/jimcrow/ stories_events_smith.html (accessed March 31, 2005).

p. 65, "I feel the Association . . ." Ransby, *Ella Baker and the Black Freedom Movement,* 146.

p. 65, "All of us here . . ." Ibid., 147.

p. 65-66, "It made me sick . . ." Grant, *Ella Baker,* 86.

p. 66, "I shall keep faith . . ." Ibid., 83.

p. 66, "She thought that every . . ." Dallard, *Ella Baker: A Leader Behind the Scenes,* 52.

p. 66, "She was very firm . . ." Ibid.

p. 67, "On one occasion . . ." Ibid., 53.

p. 70-71, "It's about time . . ." "Journey of Reconciliation," Spartacus Educational, http://www.spartacus.schoolnet.co.uk /USAjor.htm (accessed March 31, 2005).

p. 71, "America cannot . . ." Grant, *Ella Baker,* 67.

CHAPTER FIVE: Legislative Victories

p. 74, "place[d] the Negro in an . . ." Rosalind Rosenberg, "Discovering Jane Crow," Columbia University, http:// www.columbia.edu/~rr91/3567_lectures/ discovering_jane_crow.htm (accessed March 31, 2005).

p. 76, "of similar age and . . ." Ibid.

p. 76, "The United States . . ." Wexler, *The Civil Rights Movement: An Eyewitness History,* 47.

p. 76, "Even though it was . . ." PBS, "People and Events: *Brown v. Board of Education* (1954)," American Experience: The Murder of Emmett Till, 1999-2001, PBS.org, http:// www.pbs.org/wgbh/amex/till/peopleevents/e_brown.html (accessed March 31, 2005).

p. 76, "the worst thing that . . ." Ibid.

p. 77, "uptown Ku Klux . . ." Wexler, *The Civil Rights Movement: An Eyewitness History,* 53.

p. 78-79, "When I was eleven . . ." "Medgar Evers" African Within, http://www.africawithin.com/bios/ medgar_evers.htm (accessed March 31, 2005).

p. 83, "We forgot about . . ." Rosa Parks, with Jim Haskins, *Rosa Parks: My Story* (New York: Dial Books, 1992), 105-06.

p. 83, "After all, who . . ." Ransby, *Ella Baker and the Black*

Freedom Movement, 173.

p. 83-84, "I did not just . . ." Ibid., 174.

p. 84, "violate the due . . ." Wexler, *The Civil Rights Movement, An Eyewitness History,* 74.

p. 84, "thousands of individuals . . ." Ransby, *Ella Baker and the Black Freedom Movement,* 162.

CHAPTER SIX: Going South

p. 86, "political arm of . . ." Ibid., 175.

p. 86, "Not one hair of one head . . ." *New Georgia Encyclopedia,* "Ralph Abernathy (1926-1990)," http://www.georgiaencyclopedia.org/nge/ArticlePrintable.jsp?id=h-2736.

p. 88, "a spiritual assembly . . ." Ransby, *Ella Baker and the Black Freedom Movement,* 177.

p. 89, "there's not enough troops . . ." Wikipeida, "Strom Thurmond," http://en.wikipedia.org/wiki/Strom_Thurmond (accessed on March 31, 2005).

p. 91, "challenge blacks to take . . ." Ransby, *Ella Baker and the Black Freedom Movement,* 178.

p. 92, "Someone [had] . . ." Ibid., 176.

p. 92, "I had to function . . ." Ibid., 181.

p. 94, "knew from the . . ." Dallard, *Ella Baker: A Leader Behind the Scenes,* 77.

p. 94, "You see . . . it was . . ." Ibid., 76.

p. 94, "group-centered . . ." Grant, *Ella Baker,* 123.

p. 94, "We are really passing . . ." Ibid., 109.

p. 94-95, "The word *crusade* . . ." Dallard, *Ella Baker: A Leader Behind the Scenes,* 72.

p. 95, "It is possible . . ." Grant, *Ella Baker,* 119.

p. 95, "could take on . . ." Ibid.

CHAPTER SEVEN: SNCC

p. 96, "I'm sorry. We don't . . ." Wexler, *The Civil Rights Movement: An Eyewitness History,* 109.

p. 96, "I beg to disagree . . ." Ibid.

p. 97-98, "We do not intend to . . ." Herschelle S. Challenor, "Rev. Martin Luther King Jr., and the Civil Rights Movement in the US: A Second Look," AfricanAmericans.com, http://www.africanamericans.com/martinlutherkingjr.htm (accessed March 31, 2005).

p. 100, "It was very obvious . . ." Dallard, *Ella Baker: A Leader Behind the Scenes,* 81.

p. 100, "The Southern Christian . . ." Ibid., 82-83.

p. 101, "Most of the youngsters . . ." Ibid. 86.

p. 101, "What was nice about . . ." Grant, *Ella Baker,* 132.

p. 101-102, "The chief emphasis . . ." Ibid. 125.

p. 102, "little trick," Dallard, *Ella Baker: A Leader Behind the Scenes,* 84.

p. 103, "Look, here's somebody . . ." Ibid.

p. 103, "I usually tried to . . ." Ibid.

p. 103, "It was Ella more than . . ." Ibid., 84-85.

p. 104, "SNCC shall . . ." Grant, *Ella Baker,* 134, 136.

p. 104, "We are all leaders," Dallard, *Ella Baker: A Leader Behind the Scenes,* 84.

p. 105, "No argument in . . ." Payne, *I've Got the Light of Freedom,* 78.

p. 107, "the guy who made . . ." Grant, *Ella Baker,* 140.

p. 107, "There was no . . ." Ransby, *Ella Baker and the Black Freedom Movement,* 305.

p. 107, "We'd sit sometimes . . ." Ibid., 362.

p. 107-108, "Whenever you want . . ." Payne, *I've Got the Light of Freedom,* 98.

p. 108, "The field staff . . ." Ransby, *Ella Baker and the Black Freedom Movement,* 280.

CHAPTER EIGHT: Freedom Rides

p. 109, "intention was to provoke . . ." Wexler, *The Civil Rights Movement: An Eyewitness History,* 114-15.

p. 111, "couldn't see their . . ." Ibid., 116.

p. 111, "it looked like a . . ." Ibid., 117.

p. 112, "The citizens of the . . ." Taylor Branch, *Parting the Waters: America in the King Years 1954-63* (New York: Simon & Schuster Inc., 1988), 427.

p. 112, "The students have . . ." Ibid., 430.

p. 112, "Yes. That's exactly . . ." Ibid.

p. 113, "The passengers are . . ." Wexler, *The Civil Rights Movement: An Eyewitness History,* 118.

p. 114-115, "sought the worst part . . ." William Heath, "The Children Bob Moses Led," LearnToQuestion.com, http://www.learntoquestion.com/seevak/groups/2001/sites/moses/archives/excerpts/Excerpt_Heath.htm (accessed March 31, 2005).

p. 115, "I keep coming . . ." Payne, *I've Got the Light of Freedom,* 106.

p. 116, "Niggers 'round here . . ." Ibid., 248.

p. 117-118, "*Greenwood, Mississippi . . .*" Grant, *Ella Baker,* 153.

p. 120, ". . . when you have . . ." Branch, *Parting the Waters,* 739.

p. 121, "They've turned the . . ." Ibid., 759.

p. 122, "Now I've seen everything . . ." Steven Kasher, *The Civil Rights Movement: A Photographic History, 1954-68* (New York: Abbeville Press, 1996), 95.

p. 123-124, "We preach freedom . . ." Ibid., 98.

p. 124, "We owe them . . ." Branch, *Parting the Waters,* 824.

p. 124, "I may lose . . ." Ibid., 839.

CHAPTER NINE: Getting Out the Vote

p. 127-128, "I have seen people . . ." Payne, *I've Got the Light of Freedom,* 253.

p. 130, "Fellow Americans, we . . ." A. Philip Randolph, "The March on Washington Speech" The White House Historical Association, http://www.whitehousehistory.org/04/subs/activities_03/d04_01.html (accessed on March 31, 2005).

p. 130, "By the force of our . . ." Ibid.

p. 130, "I have a dream . . ." Dallard, *Ella Baker: A Leader Behind the Scenes,* 99.

p. 132, "gavel to gavel," Wexler, *The Civil Rights Movement: An Eyewitness History,* 119.

p. 132-133, "One of the reasons . . ." Ransby, *Ella Baker and the Black Freedom Movement,* 322.

p. 133-134, "came to the conclusion . . ." Dallard, *Ella Baker: A Leader Behind the Scenes,* 103.

p. 134, "Mississippi is not . . ." Kasher, *The Civil Rights Movement,* 199.

p. 134, "I may be killed . . ." Ibid.

p. 135, "The unfortunate . . ." Dallard, *Ella Baker: A Leader Behind the Scenes,* 104.

p. 137, "bill to restrain . . ." Kasher, *The Civil Rights Movement,* 199.

p. 138, "[We] believe in the segregation . . ." Grant, *Ella Baker,* 169.

p. 138, "demand to be let . . ." Nick Kotz, *Judgment Days* (Boston: Houghton Mifflin Company, 2005), 189.

p. 139, "They set me free . . ." Kate Tuttle, "Fannie Lou Hamer," Encarta Africana, http://www.africana.com/research/encarta/tt_647.asp (accessed March 31, 2005).

p. 140, "Three white men . . ." "Fannie Lou Hamer, 1917-1977" University of Houston, http://vi.uh.edu/pages/buzzmat/fannielou.html (accessed March 31, 2005).

p. 140, "Is this America? . . ." Grant, *Ella Baker,* 174.

p. 141, "To disregard the Negro's . . ." Kotz, *Judgment Days,* 190-191.

CHAPTER TEN: Fundi

p. 148, "It's a moment in history . . ." Kasher, *The Civil Rights Movement,* 221.

p. 149, "It's wrong—deadly wrong . . ." Ibid., 222.

p. 149, "Even if we pass this . . ." Ibid.

p. 150, "The law is clear . . ." "Selma-to-Montgomery March, National Historic Trail & All-American Road," We Shall Overcome, Historic Places of the Civil Rights Movement, National Park Service, http://www.cr.nps.gov/nr/travel/ civilrights/sitelist1.htm (accessed March 31, 2005).

p. 155, "I hit him. But . . ." Grant, *Ella Baker,* 211.

p. 155-156, "I was never working . . ." Ibid., 224-25.

p. 156, "If there is any . . ." Ransby, *Ella Baker and the Black Freedom Movement,* 357.

p. 156, "I believe that the . . ." Ibid., 356.

p. 156, "crusading proportions," Grant, *Ella Baker,* 199.

Bibliography

"American Experience: The Murder of Emmett Till," PBS Online, 1999-2001, http://www.pbs.org/wgbh/amex/till.

Branch, Taylor. *Parting the Waters: America in the King Year 1954-63*. New York: Simon & Schuster Inc., 1988.

———. *Pillar of Fire: American in the King Years 1963-65*. New York: Simon & Schuster Inc., 1998.

Challenor, Herschelle S. "Rev. Martin Luther King, Jr., and the Civil Rights Movement in the US: A Second Look," Americans.net, 1997-2004, http://www.africanamericans.com/martinlutherkingjr.htm.

Cohen, Lizabeth. "Black Power of the Purse." From *A Consumers' Republic: The Politics of Mass Communication in Postwar America*." Mindfully.org. http://www.mindfully.org/Reform/2003/Black-Power-PurseJan03.htm.

Coombs, Norman. *The Black Experience in America: The Immigrant Heritage of America* (1993). University of Southern California. http://www.usc.edu/isd/archives/ethnicstudies/historicdocs/Coombs/coombs_chap8.txt.

Cozzens, Lisa, "Welcome to African American History!, Mississippi & Freedom Summer," (1998; 2004) www.watson.org/~lisa/blackhistory/index.html.

Dallard, Shyrlee. *Ella Baker: A Leader Behind the Scenes*. Englewood Cliffs, NJ: Silver Burdett Press, Inc., 1990.

Du Bois, W. E. B. *Black Reconstruction in America, 1860-1880*. New York: Simon & Schuster Inc., 1995.

Encyclopedia Britannica Online. "National Council of Negro Women." Women in American. http://www.britannica.com/women/articles/National_Council_of_Negro_Women.html.

Grant, Joanne. *Ella Baker: Freedom Bound.* New York: John Wiley & Sons, Inc., 1998.

Hamer, Fannie Lou. "Fannie Lou Hamer, 1917-1977" University of Houston, http://vi.uh.edu/pages/buzzmat/fannielou.html.

Heath, William. "The Children Bob Moses Led." LearnToQuestion.com. http://www.learntoquestion.com/seevak/groups/2001/sites/moses/archives/excerpts/Excerpt_Heath.htm.

Kasher, Steven. *The Civil Rights Movement: A Photographic History, 1954-68.* New York: Abbeville Press, 1996.

King, Mary. *Freedom Song: A Personal Story of the 1960s Civil Rights Movement.* New York: William Morrow and Company, Inc., 1987.

Kotz, Nick. *Judgment Days.* Boston: Houghton Mifflin, 2005.

Look magazine. "The Shocking Story of Approved Killing in Mississippi." PBS Online, American Experience: The Murder of Emmett Till, http://www.pbs.org/wgbh/amex/till/sfeature/sf_look_confession.html.

Lyon, Danny. *Memories of the Southern Civil Rights Movement.* Chapel Hill: Center for Documentary Studies, Duke University by The University of North Carolina Press, 1992.

"Medgar Evers." African Within. http://www.africawithin.com/bios/medgar_evers.htm.

Moore, Charles (photography) and Michael S. Durham (text). *Powerful Days: The Civil Rights Photography of Charles Moore.* Tuscaloosa: The University of Alabama Press, 1991.

National Park Service. "Selma-to-Montgomery March, National Historic Trail & All-American Road," http://www.cr.nps.gov/nr/travel/civilrights/sitelist1.htm.

New Georgia Encyclopedia. "Ralph Abernathy (1926-1990)." http://www.georgiaencyclopedia.org/nge/ ArticlePrintable.jsp?id=h-2736.

Parks, Rosa, with Jim Haskins. *Rosa Parks: My Story.* New York: Dial Books, 1992.

Payne, Charles M. *I've Got the Light of Freedom: The Organizing Tradition and the Mississippi Freedom Struggle.* Berkeley: University of California Press, 1995.

"People and Events: *Brown v. Board of Education* 1954," *American Experience: The Murder of Emmett Till, 1999-2001,* PBS Online, http://www.pbs.org/wgbh/amex/till/ peopleevents/e_brown.html.

Randolph, A. Philip. "The March on Washington Speech." The White House Historical Association, http://www. whitehousehistory.org/04/subs/activities_03/d04_01.html.

Ransby, Barbara. *Ella Baker and the Black Freedom Movement, A Radical Democratic Vision.* Chapel Hill, North Carolina: The University of North Carolina Press, 2003.

Rosenberg, Rosalind. "Discovering Jane Crow." Columbia University, http://www.columbia.edu/~rr91/3567_lectures/ discovering_jane_crow.htm.

Schultz, Stanley K. "Lecture 09: The Great Migration: Blacks in White America." American History 102: Civil War to the Present, University of Wisconsin, http://us.history.wisc.edu/ hist102/lectures/lecture09.html.

Spartacus Educational. "Journey of Reconciliation." http:// www.spartacus.schoolnet.co.uk/USAjor.htm.

Tuttle, Kate. "Fannie Lou Hamer." Encarta Africana. http:// www.africana.com/research/encarta/tt_647.asp.

Wexler, Sanford. *The Civil Rights Movement, An Eyewitness History.* New York: Facts On File, 1993.

Wormser, Richard. "The Rise and Fall of Jim Crow." PBS.org. http://www.pbs.org/wnet/jimcrow/stories_events_ww2.html.

Web sites

http://www.ellabakercenter.org/index.html
The Ella Baker Center for Human Rights is located in Oakland, California, and is named in honor of Baker's contributions to fighting injustice.

http://www.naacp.org/
The online home of the NAACP.

http://www.thebakerhouse.org/
Named in honor of Ella Baker, the Baker House's motto is, "Transforming Inner City Neighborhoods One Child at a Time."

http://www.ncsu.edu/chass/mds/ellahome.html
North Carolina State University hosted a conference in April 2000 to commemorate the fortieth anniversary of the founding of SNCC and Ella Baker's contributions to the civil rights movement.

http://sclcnational.org/
The online home of the SCLC.

Index